Ya no sé si maldecirte o por ti rezar

Paloma negra,
paloma negra,

¿dónde, dónde andarás?

Ya no juegues con mi honra,
parrandera

Si tus caricias han de ser mías, de nadie más

black dove

ana castillo

black dove
mamá, mi'jo, and me

FEMINIST
PRESS
AT THE CITY UNIVERSITY
OF NEW YORK
NEW YORK CITY

Published in 2016 by the Feminist Press
at the City University of New York
The Graduate Center
365 Fifth Avenue, Suite 5406
New York, NY 10016

feministpress.org

First Feminist Press edition 2016

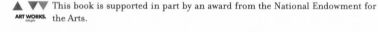 This book is supported in part by an award from the National Endowment for the Arts.

 This book was made possible thanks to a grant from New York State Council on the Arts with the support of Governor Andrew Cuomo and the New York State Legislature.

Third printing April 2019

Cover photo and design by Drew Stevens
Text design by Suki Boynton

Library of Congress Cataloging-in-Publication Data
Names: Castillo, Ana, author.
Title: Black dove : essays on mama, mi'jo, and me / Ana Castillo.
Description: New York : The Feminist Press at CUNY, 2016.
Identifiers: LCCN 2015048671 | ISBN 9781558619234 (paperback)
Subjects: LCSH: Castillo, Ana. | Castillo, Ana—Family. | Mexican American women authors—20th century—Biography. | Mothers and daughters—United States—Biography. | Mexican American families—Biography. | Mexican Americans—Social conditions—20th century. | BISAC: BIOGRAPHY & AUTOBIOGRAPHY / Personal Memoirs. | FAMILY & RELATIONSHIPS / Parenting / Motherhood. | FAMILY & RELATIONSHIPS / Parenting / Single Parent. | BIOGRAPHY & AUTOBIOGRAPHY / Cultural Heritage.
Classification: LCC PS3553.A8135 Z46 2016 | DDC 814/.54—dc23
LC record available at https://lccn.loc.gov/2015048671

Contents

To all those who dare to dream—not necessarily for riches and fame—but for everyone on the planet to live with dignity.

And to the loves of my life, my children: Marcel and Mariana Castillo.

May the future always hold for them grace and joy.

*My grandparents María de Jesús and Santos Rocha
and their son, Rudolfo.*

Introduction

Perhaps some of you may come away from this book feeling that my stories have nothing to do with your lives. You may find the interest I've had in my ancestors as they were shaped by the politics of their times, irrelevant to your own history. My story, as a brown, bisexual, strapped writer and mother, constantly scrambling to take care of my work and my child, might be similarly inconsequential. However, I beg your indulgence and a bit of faith to believe that maybe on the big Scrabble board of life we will eventually cross ways and make sense to each other.

If you reside in the United States, whether you are able to vote or pay taxes, then know that you and I have much more in common than not. Know that we may differ greatly in opinion, but only a handful in the world make decisions that affect the majority, and that majority includes you and me. If we question what passes for truth or the veracity of any point of view, these days bombarded and overloaded as we are with random sound bites, know also that knowledge sets you free. Knowledge makes you strong. Not scatter-shot information gleaned off the Internet or the opinions of Facebook friends, but checking and cross-checking your resources, going to the source, radical curiosity—that kind of knowledge.

I focus my observations on my own background because it has been critical throughout my life to find out who I am. You see, I never saw *me* in history books. I didn't find women who looked like me in the Edna St. Vincent Millay sonnets I fell in love with at sixteen in my secretarial school's library. That wasn't me or my mother in the paintings I studied at my beloved Art Institute of Chicago. I didn't see us on television or at the symphony or the ballet. We weren't in white smocks in hospitals or running for office. In public schools, I grew up without a single Latino instructor with whom to identify; indeed, I had none in college. The Latino student organization I participated in demanded a Chicano instructor and we finally prevailed in my last year, welcoming a young ABD sociologist not much older than those of us he'd teach. And yes, having that changed my life. What I heard in his class left me astounded and affirmed.

You may be interested in math and science or business and profit. You might want to work with destitute children in faraway places, or you may be wishing for the chance to make enough money to buy your mother a home someday to say you achieved your dream. We all aspire to something, which is why we are here. The dreams vary, but we remain in the same world at the same time. My message to you, the next generation of dreamers, begins with a summary of an earlier generation—not mine, but that of my grandmother.

We all know that this young and mighty country in which we live was built on the literal blood, sweat, and tears of many people from diverse backgrounds and places. The United States is a young country, because in comparison to civilizations that go back millennia—Egypt, China, Japan, the Incas, Rome—it is a scant couple hundred plus change years old. When it was about half its age, right before the twentieth century, there was great energy and excitement in building a railroad system that would revolutionize exports and imports and continue this country's prosperity. The president of México and the US government worked jointly on this effort. It was a time of enormous gains for the United States. For México, not so much—except for the few in power who became rich. Then they had a civil war. As a result of the Mexican Revolution a hundred years ago, my paternal ancestors migrated north and settled in Chicago. My father was born in that city of unforgiving winters and steamy beach summers, asphalt all around and the factories that Jane Addams so protested, the reeking slaughterhouse on Halsted and black fume-releasing oil refineries and the steel mills of the South Side. I was born in the same city and grew up in the same neighborhood as he had.

My mother's father was from Guanajuato, México. He was a signalman with the railroad and part of the great frenzy of prospering times. We like to say in this country that if you work hard you can have a piece of the pie. Apparently, he got his, traveling with his young bride, sometime around 1918, north, where they lived for seven years before their first child was born in Kansas. I have pictures in my study of my lovely grandmother in her wide-brimmed hat, chemise dress, and pearls, and my grandfather with his handlebar mustache and pocket watch, in front of their car. Their son posed in a photo studio in his tweed suit and cap. My mother came along two years later in Nebraska in 1927. There are sepia pictures of her, too. Sweet. The infant is sitting up with a knitted sweater over her pretty dress. Had the mother made it for her child? Did she find the day too chilled in Nebraska and fear her baby might catch a draft?

As you may know (or not, I will tell you anyway) the history of the country includes the liberal importation of labor during times of growth. My grandparents were a part of this migration. The European settlers had suppressed, enslaved, and eliminated indigenous peoples; the survivors were sent to reservations. This is not the old days, or once-upon-a-time talk. We still have reservations in this country. They are not on the most fertile lands. Poverty and all the stigmas that affect demeaned communities are present. High suicide and drug rates hobble the youth in an already dwindling population. Let's take a second to think about that reality— tracts of depleted land for the original peoples of this land. And consider, too, the slave labor brought from across the seas. Even the Emancipation Proclamation of 1863 did not fully bring former slaves into the democratic fold.

At the end of the nineteenth century and the start of the next, Mexicans had their own dark history with the US government. At that time, they were willing, eager, and able to lay down tracks and pick cotton. Mind you, the Border Patrol wasn't established until 1924, so people came back and forth freely. In fact, the Border Patrol wasn't established at first to keep out Mexicans. The Chinese Exclusion Act of 1882 was passed by Congress to prevent immigration from China via México. This was the first significant law restricting immigration to the United States.

But wait, a lot of people were coming in at that time. They came with whatever they had in their hands and on their backs, along with their dreams, to Ellis Island. Throughout the eighteenth and nineteenth centuries and into the early decades of the twentieth century, new Europeans arrived and were faced with animosity. Historians have documented the racist and ethnic prejudices that each group experienced for at least a generation before assimilating. "Everyone had to pay his or her dues" before being allowed entry into the American Club, as the adage went.

Ellis Island in New York was the destination point for a second wave of immigration from 1892 to 1954. But decades before Ellis Island opened as a processing center, New York had already received around eight million immigrants. The Great Potato Famine caused many Irish to immigrate to the

United States in the mid-nineteenth century. Legislature denied entrance to a few—convicts, "lunatics and idiots," people with no means to take care of themselves, prostitutes, labor brokers, the Chinese—in other words, the usual suspects.

If you were more or less healthy and could prove you would not be a burden on society, you got to stay. Conveniently, on the East Coast, the Germans and Irish (who were not part of the Anglo-Saxon political elite) were able to expedite citizenship at voting time and gain full entrance into society. Approximately twenty to thirty thousand men (and their families) were naturalized in New York City in 1868 alone in the weeks before that year's presidential election. Briefly, in the eighteenth century, after five years of residence, European arrivals could apply for citizenship and, in fact, when they first arrived, were encouraged to do so as part of their assimilation.

Earlier, around 1840, lawmakers in Washington turned their sights to the vast territories of the Southwest pertaining to México, justifying their dreams for grandiosity with the ideology of Manifest Destiny. An invasion was executed, followed by a brief war and a surrender. Half of México became part of the United States in 1848. To coax people to establish the West, the government sold land cheaply to citizens and European immigrants alike. Long-established hacendados, ranchers, and landowners—formerly Mexican—often lost their properties in strange maneuvers manipulated by the new government.

Fast-forward seventy yea. , zooming prosperity came to a sudden halt with the Stock Market Crash of 1929. The country could not sustain itself. The Great Depression began. Measures were taken and the labor provided by Mexicans was undesired. The nation needed rescuing, and it was thought then that Mexic ns and US citizens of Mexican descent shouldn't just get in t. ck of the line, they should leave altogether. Vamos. The Immigration and Naturalization Service (INS) was determined to "repatriate" Mexicans and their American-born children. Sometimes they did it with a train ticket, others were pressured and threatened. Sixty percent of those deported were American citizens. Undergoing its own economic crisis, the Mexican government was unable to accommodate or provide for these repatriated families, so recently part of the American Dream. It has been estimated by historians and acknowledged by US Citizenship and Immigration Services that in the two years after the crash, at least two hundred thousand Mexicans left the United States. Over the next ten years, altogether an estimated four hundred thousand to one million Mexicans and Mexican Americans were deported to México.

Soon after my maternal family was repatriated, my mother's father died. When my mother was nine, her mother, too, passed, most likely of tuberculosis, leaving her an orphan. She, along with her brother, Tío Leonel, and sister, Tía Flora, and other cousins affected by the repatriation, lived with their grandparents, people of humble means. My mother, an American citizen born in a middle-class home in the Midwest, found herself now growing up in México. Without other options, she went to work as a live-in servant. Years later, the grandparents brought the young-adult grandchildren as far as the border, encouraged their return to the United States to find work, and hoped for the best.

My mother lived and worked in Chicago for the rest of her life. But, a funny thing, I never knew her to speak English. She had mostly worked in factories, on assembly lines. Foremen were gringos—she had to understand some English. My parents subscribed to the *Chicago Sun-Times*, which she read. She sold Avon for thirty-eight years, until her death. Still, her refusal to speak English at home convinced me that she didn't understand. "¿Qué? No te entiendo," she'd say to me.

To think that less than a hundred years ago, up to a million people were corralled, harassed, and handed orders as private citizens to leave this country. They were told to leave hard-earned good lives behind, lives that might've included work, property, family, community, church, and future plans. This seems a monumentally sad, unimaginative way to fix a fallen economy.

¿Qué? No lo entiendo, I say to you.

Flora, Leonel, and Mamá (Mexico City; approximately 1938).

My Mother's México

My mother's México was the brutal urban reality of Luis Buñuel's *Los Olvidados*. Children scamming and hustling, fire-eaters, hubcap stealers, Chiclet sellers, miniature accordion players with small, dirty hands stretched out before passersby for a coin, a piece of bread: "Please, señor, for my mother who is very sick." This was the Mexico City of my family. This was the México from which my mother spared me.

In that Mexico City in the 1930s, Mamá was a street urchin with one ragged dress—but not an orphan, not yet. Because of an unnamed skin disease that covered her whole tiny body with scabs, her head was shaved. At seven years old, or maybe eight, she scurried, quick and invisible as a Mayan messenger, through the throngs of that ancient metropolis in the area known as "La Villita," where the goddess Guadalupe Tonantzin had made her four divine appearances and ordered el indio Juan Diego four times to tell the Catholic officials to build her a church. "Yes!"

and off he went, sure-footed and trembling. Mamá, who was not Mamá but little then, bustled on her own mission toward the corner where her stepfather sold used paperbacks on the curb. At midday he ordered his main meal from a nearby restaurant and ate it out of stainless-steel carryout containers without leaving his place of business. The little girl would take the leftovers and dash them off to her mother, who was lying on a petate—in the one room the whole family shared in a vecindad overflowing with families like their own with all manner of maladies that accompany destitution. Her mother was dying.

María de Jesús Rocha de Castro spent her days and nights in the dark, windowless room reading novels, used paperbacks provided by her new husband from Veracruz, seconds like the food he shared with her. She copied favorite passages and verses into a notebook, which I have inherited, not through the pages of a will but by my mother's will: she carried the notebook, preserved in its faded newsprint cover, over decades of migration until, one day, it was handed over to me, the daughter who also liked to read, to write, to save things.

María de Jesús named her second daughter after a fictional character, Florinda, but my mother was the eldest daughter. She was not named for romance like my tía Flora—aromatic and evocative—but from the Old Testament, Raquel, a name as impenetrable as the rock in her parents' shared Guanajuatan family name, Rocha: Raquel Rocha

Rocha. And quite a rock my ˌ ˌ ˌ ˌ ˌ ˌ er was all the days of her life, Moses and Mount Sinai and God striking lightning all over the place, Raquel the Rock.

One day, María de Jesús—the maternal grandmother whom I never knew but was told I am so much like—asked her eldest daughter to purchase a harmonica for her. Of course, it would be a cheap one that could be obtained from a street vendor not unlike her bookselling husband. This the child did, and brought it to her mother's deathbed, a straw mat on a stone floor. And when the mother felt well enough, she produced music out of the little instrument, in the dark of that one room in Mexico City, the city where she had gone with her parents and two eldest children with the hope of getting good medical care that could rarely be found in those days outside the capital.

Instead, María stood in line outside a dispensary. Dispensaries were medical clinic substitutes, equipped to offer little more than drugs, certain common injections, and lightweight medical advice. In a rosary chain of women like herself—black rebozos, babies at the breast—she waited for hours in the sun or rain, on the ground. So many lives and that woman at the end, there, yes, that one, my mother's young mother waited, dying.

In the 1970s while I was living alone in Mexico City, I had a medical student friend who took me to such a dispensary where he worked most evenings. The place, located in a poor colonia, consisted of two dark rooms—one for the receptionist and the other for consultation. The dispensary was crammed to the ceiling with boxes of drugs, mostly from the United States, administered freely to patients. I knew almost nothing about medication, but I knew that in the United States we did not have a once-a-month birth control pill, and that belladonna could not be taken without a doctor's prescription. And yet, drugs such as these were abundant in the dispensary, and my young friend was not a doctor but, in fact, was a failing medical school student, permitted to prescribe at his own discretion.

María de Jesús was newly widowed during her dispensary days, and why she married again so soon (the bookseller) I cannot say, except that she was so sick—and with two children—that shelter and leftovers may have been reason enough. She bore two children quickly from this second marriage, unlike the first, in which, among other differences, it took seven years before the couple had their first child, a son born in Kansas, and two years later a daughter, my mother, born in Nebraska.

My mother often told me my grandfather worked on the railroads as a signalman. This is what brought the Guanajuatan couple to the United States. From this period—the 1920s—I can construct a biography of the couple myself because María de Jesús was very fond of being photographed. She wore fine silks and chiffons and wide-brimmed hats. Her mustached husband with the heavy-lidded eyes telling of his Indian ancestry sported a gold pocket watch. They drove a Studebaker.

After the Stock Market Crash of 1929, Mexican workers in the United States, suddenly jobless, were quickly returned to the other side of the border. My grandparents returned not with severance pay, not with silk dresses nor wool suits, not with the Studebaker—but with tuberculosis. My grandfather died soon after.

When María de Jesús died (not surprisingly, she was not saved by the rudimentary medical treatment she received at dispensaries), her children—two sons, two daughters—were sent out to work to earn their own keep. Where the sons went, I don't know as much. But I know about the daughters—Raquel and her younger sister, Flora—because when they grew up and became women, they told me in kitchens, over meals, and into late evenings, that by the time they were ten years old, they worked as live-in domestics.

My mother was a little servant. Perhaps that is why later, when she became a wife and mother, she kept a neat home. My tía Flora was sent to the kitchen of an Arab family. And in adulthood, her tiny flat was always crowded, filled with crazy chaos, as she became the best Mexican cook on both sides of the border. It was a veritable Tenochtitlán feast at Flora's table in her humble casita at the outpost of Mesoamerica—that is to say, the mero corazón of the Mexican barrio of Chicago: spices and sauces of cumin and sesame seeds, chocolate, ground peanuts, and all varieties of chiles; cuisines far from shy or hesitant, but bold and audacious, of fish, fowl, and meats. Feasts fit for a queen.

When my mother was about seventeen, her guardian

grandparents decided to take their US-born grandchildren closer to the border. The strategy of the migrating abuelos was that the US-born grandchildren could get better work or, at least, perhaps better pay on the US side. They settled in Nuevo Laredo. One year later, my mother was raped—or at a minimum clearly taken advantage of—by the owner of the restaurant on the US side of the border where she had found work as a waitress. (She never said which it was, or at least, she never told me.) He was married with a family and considerably older than the teenager who bore his son. The best my great-grandfather could do at that point on behalf of my mother's honor was to get the man to provide for her. He paid the rent on a little one-room wooden house, which, of course, gave him further claims on my mother. Two years later, a daughter was born.

Three years more and Mamá's México ended as a daily construct of her reality when, with machete in hand, she went out to make her own path. She left her five-year-old son with her sister Flora, who was newlywed (and soon to be widowed), and, with her three-year-old girl, followed some cousins who had gone up north. A year later, she would move to Chicago alone with both children. Mamá remembers all this as the longest year of her life.

In Chicago, my mother went to work in factories. Doña Jovita, the curandera who took care of Mamá's two children while she worked, convinced the young mother to marry her teenage son. The next summer, I was born. Mamá stayed in factories until the last one closed up and packed off to Southeast Asia, leaving its union workers without work and some without pensions, and sending my mother into early retirement.

Mamá, a dark mestiza, inherited the complexes and fears of the colonized and the strange sense of national pride that permeates the new society of the conquered. Although she lived in Chicago for over forty years, she spoke only Spanish. She threw out English words—*zas, zas, zas*—like stray bullets leveled at gringos, at grandchildren, at her African American Avon manager.

When I was twelve, I saw Mamá's Mexico City for the first time. My mother and I traveled from Chicago to Nuevo Laredo by car. It was possibly the hottest place on earth in the month of July. Mamá didn't have much choice about when to travel, since the first two weeks of July were when the factory where she worked closed down and workers were given vacation time. Mamá paid a young Mexican who was looking for riders to take us to the border. The car broke down, we slept in it at night, we were refused service at gas stations and in restaurants in the South. Finally, we got to my great-grandmother's two-room wooden house with an outhouse and a shower outside.

I had made friends with the little girl next door, Rosita, on a previous visit to Nuevo Laredo. At that time, we climbed trees and fed the chickens and took sides with each other against her older brother. That's how and why I learned to write Spanish, to write to my friend. My mother said it was also to exchange letters with Mamá Grande, my mother's grandmother, but I wanted to keep up with Rosita. My mother, after long days at the factory, would come home to make dinner, and after the dishes and just before bed, she, with her sixth-grade education and admirable penmanship, would sit me down at the kitchen table and teach me how to write in Spanish, phonetically, with soft vowels, with humor, with a pencil, and with no book.

On the next visit, Rosita was fourteen. She had crossed over to that place of no return—breasts and boys. Her dark cheeks were flushed all the time, and in place of the two thick plaits with red ribbons she once wore, she now left her hair loose down her back. She didn't want to climb trees anymore. I remember a quiet, tentative conversation in the bedroom she shared with her grandmother who had raised her. Not long after that, Rosita ran off—with whom, where, or what became of her life, I was never to know.

In Nuevo Laredo we were met by my tía Flora—who had also traveled from Chicago—with her five children, ranging from ages fourteen to four. The husbands of these two sisters did not come along on this pilgrimage because they were men who, despite having families, were not family men. They passed up their traditional right to accompany their wives and children on the temporary repatriation.

There were too many children to sleep in the house, so we were sent up to the flat roof to sleep under the stars. My mother had not known that she needed permission from my father to take me into México, so with my cousin's birth certificate to pass me off as Mexican-born, we all got on a train one day, and I illegally entered Mexico City.

Our life in Chicago was not suburban backyards with swings and grassy lawns. It was not what I saw on TV. And yet it was not the degree of poverty in which we all found ourselves immersed overnight, through inheritance, birth, bad luck, or destiny. It was the destiny that my mother and her sister had dodged by doing as their mother, María de Jesús, had done decades before (for a period of her life at least) by getting the hell out of México, however they could. It was destiny in México that my mother's little brother refused to reject because of his hatred for capitalism, which he felt was embodied by the United States. Leonel came out of the México of Diego and Frida and was a proud communist. Dark and handsome in his youth, with thin lips that curled up, giving him the permanent expression of a cynic, the brother left behind came to get us at the little hotel in Mexico City where my mother's stepfather, who was still selling books on a street corner, had installed us the night before. He'd met us at the train station, feeding us all bowls of atole for our late meal at the restaurant where his credit was good.

My cousin Sandra and I opened the door for Tío Leonel. We didn't know who he was. We told him our mothers had gone on an errand, taking the younger children with them. My tío Leonel did not step all the way into the room. We were young females alone, and for him to do so would have been improper. He looked me up and down with black eyes as black as my mother's, as black as mine, and knitted eyebrows as serious as Mamá's and as serious as mine were to become.

"You are Raquel's daughter?" he asked. I nodded. And then he left.

He returned for us later, Mamá and me and my tía Flora and her five children, eight of us all together, plus big suitcases, and took us to his home. Home for Tío Leonel was a dark room in a vecindad. Vecindades are communal living quarters. Families stay in single rooms. They share toilet and water facilities. The women have a tiny closet for a kitchen just outside their family's room, and they cook on a griddle on the floor. I don't remember my uncle's common-law wife's name. I am almost certain that it was María, but that would be a lucky guess. I remember my cousins who were all younger than me and their cuh-razy chilango accents. But I don't remember their names or how many there were then. There were nearly ten—but not ten yet—because that would be the total number my uncle and his woman would eventually have. Still, it felt like ten. So now there were four adults and at least thirteen children, age fourteen and under, staying in one room.

We didn't have to worry about crowding the bathroom because the toilets were already shared by the entire vecindad. There were no lights and no plumbing. At night sometimes my uncle cleverly brought in an electrical line from outside and connected a bulb. This was not always possible or safe. The sinks used for every kind of washing were unsanitary. Sandra and I went to wash our hands and faces one morning and both stepped back at the sight of a very ugly black fish that had burst out of the drainpipe and was swimming around in the large plugged-up basin.

For entertainment, we played balero with our cousins who were experts. Balero was a handheld toy where the object of the game was to flip a wooden ball on a string onto a peg. My little cousins could not afford a real balero, even the cheap kind you find in abundance in colorful mercados, and made their own using cans, found string, and stones or cork.

A neighbor in the vecindad who owned the local candy stand had a black-and-white portable TV. At a certain hour every evening, she charged the children who could afford it to sit in the store to watch their favorite cartoon show.

I was twelve years old, Sandra was thirteen, and her older brother was fourteen. We were beyond cartoon shows and taking balero contests seriously, and we were talking our early teen talk to each other in English. It was 1965 and the Rolling Stones were singing "(I Can't Get No) Satisfaction" in English over Spanish radio on my cousin's made-in-Japan transistor, and we insolent US-born adolescents wanted no part of México. Not the México of the amusement park, La Montaña Rusa, where we went one day and had great fun on the roller coaster. No. the México of sleeping under the stars on the roof of my tío Aurelio's home in Nuevo Laredo. Not the México of the splendid gardens of Chapultepec Park, of the cadet heroes, Los Niños Héroes, who valiantly but fatally fought off the invasion of US troops. We wanted no part of *this* México, where we all slept on the mattress our mothers had purchased for us on the first night in my tío Leonel's home. It was laid out in the middle of the room, and six children and two grown women slept on it crossways, lined up neatly like soldiers on the front line at night in the trenches, head-to-toe, head-to-toe. My tío and his wife and children all slept around us on piles of rags.

We had, with one train ride, stepped right into our mothers' México, unchanged in the nearly two decades since their departure.

Years later, when I was living on my own in California, I met my family at the appointed meeting place—my tío Aurelio's in Nuevo Laredo—and traveled south by van with everybody to Mexico City. My tía Flora, this time without any of her children, came along, too. It was 1976, the birthday of the United States, but in México my elders were all dying. The great-grandmother, Apolinar, had died earlier that same year and we had only recently received word of it. The great-uncle and border official, Tío Aurelio, had a heart condition and also died before this visit. My tía Flora's veracruzano bookselling father had died that year, too. We had only the little brother Leonel to visit. The young anticapitalista—once so proud of his sole possession (a new bicycle, which eventually was stolen), devoted to his family in his own way (although the older children had gone off on their own, while the youngest sold Chiclets on the streets)— was on his deathbed at forty.

Leonel was suffering from a corroded liver, cirrhosis ridden. By then, his lot had improved so that he had two rooms, a real bed, and electricity, but not much more. We stood around his bed and visited awhile so he could meet his brother-in-law and some other members of my mother's family whom he had never known before.

We went to visit his oldest daughter, around my age, at the house where she worked as a live-in domestic. She could not receive company, of course, but was allowed to visit with us outside for a bit. We dropped in on her older brother, too. He had an honest-to-goodness apartment—three whole rooms and its own kitchen. All grown, he worked in a factory and had a young family of his own.

One evening, my tía Flora and I ran into Leonel on the street, not far from where the cousin with the apartment lived. He was now a yellowish wire of a man and appeared quite drunk, his pants held up by a rope. He glanced at me, and then asked my tía Flora, "Is this Raquel's daughter?" My tía, in her usual happy-sounding way, said, "Yes, yes, of course she is the hija of Raquel." And then Tía, who is more veracruzana than chilanga—that is, more palm than granite—laughed a summer-rainstorm laugh.

Of course I was and am the daughter of Raquel. But I was

the one born so far north that not only my tío but all my relatives in México found it hard to think me real. The United States was Atlantis—and there was no Atlantis— and therefore having been born there, I could not exist. He nodded at my aunt, who was real, but not at me, who was a hologram, and went on his way.

"My poor brother," my tía said, "he looks like Cantinflas," comparing him to the renowned comedic actor, famous for his derelict appearance and street ways. That was the last time we saw him, and by the end of summer, he was dead.

If the double "rock" in Mamá's name (and the "castle" at the end through marriage) had dubbed her the stoic sister, the flower in Flora's name perfumed her urban life and warded off the sadness of trying times. And those had been many in my tía's life, multiplied with the years as her children grew up far from México in Chicago's poverty.

So it was that night that my tía and I, riding a city bus, jumped off suddenly in a plaza where trios and duos of musicians gathered for hire, and we brought a late-night serenade to Mamá and family at our hotel. That was when my tía Flora and I bonded as big-time dreamers. After the serenade and after Dad (who came on this trip) had brought out a bottle of mezcal and we had all shared a drink with the musicians, Mamá told me some of the stories I share here now.

By migrating, Mamá saved me from the life of a live-in domestic and perhaps from inescapable poverty in Mexico

City. But it was the perseverance of Raquel the Rock and the irrepressible sensuality of Flora the thick-stemmed calla lily that saved me, too. "Ana del Aire," my mother called me (after the popular telenovela of the 1970s). Woman of the air, not earthbound, not rooted to one place—not to México where Mamá's mother died, not to Chicago where I was born and where my mother passed away on a dialysis machine, not to New Mexico where I made a home for my son and later, alone for myself—but to everywhere at once.

And when the world so big becomes a small windowless room for me, I draw from the vision of María de Jesús. I read and write poems. I listen to music, I sing—with the voice of my ancestors from Guanajuato who had birds in their throats. I paint with my heart, with acrylics and oils on linen and cotton. On the phone, I talk to my son, to a lover, and with my comadres. I tell a story. I make a sound and leave a mark—as palatable as a prickly pear, more solid than stone.

Mamá, age 17, New Year's (Laredo, TX; 1944).

Remembering Las Cartoneras

At the turn of the century, people everywhere were making plans to travel to a place that was meaningful to them, a place that would make them feel ever so glad to be alive, witnessing the ushering in of the third millennium. Throughout the 1990s, the United States was deep in the embrace of the American Dream, and it seemed the nation had nothing but more of the same to look forward to in the new century. My tía Flora, the mother of five, grandmother of eighteen, and great-grandma to nine, who had not taken a vacation in over twenty years and had not even so much as flown on a plane before, was no exception.

In 2000, without discussing her plan with anyone (except with her late husband and my mother and father, who were her confidants in heaven now, she said), Flora booked a couple of tickets, grabbed a young grandson, and, using the stocky seven-year-old in lieu of a walker, forced her arthritic legs to board a direct flight to Mexico City—El De Efe—place of her birth.

At seventeen, my tía Flora left México. She started the march north, the same route as my mother before her, stopping for a short time in Nuevo Laredo where their grandparents had relocated. It was a strategic move to be close to the Border where their grandchildren might cross over to work. As a new bride with a Tex-Mex husband and small children in tow, Flora next traveled to Chicago and stayed for life. The city was idyllic to my aunt. It became her "Paris," she came to say as the years passed, with its pristine parks, Magnificent Mile (where a woman with little means could still window shop even if she couldn't go in to buy), its lively summer street fairs and snowy winters.

Her new husband took a job in a factory, and once all the children started school, she applied for work as a seamstress in a small upholstery company. "I'd never used a sewing machine before in my life," she told me back then, "but when the owner asked if I could handle it, I said, 'Yes, of course I could' and did. He never regretted hiring me and I never let him down. I loved all the years I worked there. I loved my fellow seamstresses, even the cheap-minded owner!"

My aunt did not use the word "love." She said "encantada," which in English means "enchanted" and which could not have been what she felt eight hours a day, the same foot pushing an industrial Singer pedal, developing arthritis, fingers pricked to the point of numbness, getting carpal tunnel syndrome as the years wore on, earnestly working toward each hour's quota. It was my tía Flora who was enchanted.

True, her whole life was devoid of privilege. She had scarcely known her mother, who died when she was but a small child. Her father eked out a living selling used books on the street, and providing for his children was impossible. She spent her adolescence as a live-in servant in Mexico City. Yet there was something about Flora that, as perfume commercials suggest about a woman with an alluring scent, emitted a touch of class, style, a dash of crimson across an otherwise gray palette. Not glamour, fancy jewelry, or extravagant parties, but a taste for life, the joie de vivre that eludes so many.

It was in the details, as I noticed even as a child when I spent a few New Year's Eves with her and my five cousins. (Where her husband was, I never knew. My own parents were out for the night—although not together). My mother, who never went out, made New Year's Eve the exception. My tía Flora, perhaps by default, was our sitter and, without a word of complaint, set a formal table for us children with the silverware in place as if we were adults and important. She served us each small portions of luxurious steak. We drank Tang or milk from her best glasses. Twelve purple grapes waited in small bowls for the striking of midnight, when each one devoured represented a wish for each month of the coming year. We couldn't afford new red underwear for good luck, but she'd given us red and yellow balloons to blow up and pins to pop them with after midnight. We each took a turn stepping out to the apartment hall and coming back in with an empty valise—to ensure a fun trip in the coming year (to children of people without automobiles and who never took vacations).

These Mexican rituals were "the way a year should start," Tía Flora thought, with the best of everything laid out and sending out all your hopes and desires. Pop, pop, pop, kiss, kiss, and kiss. What we children wished for, I don't recall. A reasonable guess would be for a bike or something along those lines. What my lovely young aunt wished for, however, I can only speculate.

Throughout the years on special occasions there were embroidered napkins at the dining-room table where Tía Flora served up exquisite meals in her tiny flat in a one-hundred-or-so-year-old brick tenement that she and her husband eventually mortgaged. The bedroom was tiny-tiny, and the back hallway ended up serving as a clothes closet and storage space. Yet, there was the wearing of a hat and gloves to church in the days of Jackie Kennedy, the elegant sling-back low heels, the margaritas Tía Flora made and served in martini glasses. When she let you hear it, her pitch-perfect singing voice—"Cucurrucucu Paloma." Where my aunt got her panache, I never knew. She simply had it.

One of my favorite stories regarding my tía Flora, who was not just my aunt but became a friend (meaning, once I was grown, we often enjoyed a good "just between us girls" laugh together), took place in the 1970s when she would have been in her forties. Tía Flora and my mother did not share the same father; their widowed mother remarried before dying young. My mother's father, from his photographs, was evidently indio. They were from the state of Guanajuato, which is inland. Tía Flora's father came from the port city of Veracruz, where ships once arrived carrying slaves from Africa. Veracruz is permeated with Caribbean culture: marimbas and fried plantains, tall "mulattos" (as they were known and how my mamá's half sister would also have been seen), and palm breezes coming in from now oil-spilled beaches.

Tía Flora inherited her father's kinky hair, which she always kept closely cropped, a look that enhanced her pretty face with the large gold hoop earrings she favored most of her life. She was certain she also got her love of music from this father she hardly knew, who gave her no reason to think so but who, she came to believe, had come to México by boat from Cuba as a young sailor or stowaway. (He did bear the same surname as the island's revolutionary dictator, after all.) Ah, what difference would it all make? Tía Flora thought, cherishing the notion of a bloodline to Havana. Before the Cuban Revolution, when Tía Flora spent her teen years working in the kitchen of a private residence in la capital, she listened to Benny Moré, Cachao López, and Miguel Matamoros, who brought their sones, boleros, and mambos from that country to México.

She was a girl dreaming like all teens dreamed, and what she began to dream about was an island where the air smelled of butterfly jasmine, young people spent their evenings sipping rum drinks from coconuts and eating guava sweets, a far-off land surrounded by salt water—nothing like the asphalt density of Mexico City, where she was born and grew into a young woman with generous hips that swished to a palm rhythm of their own when she walked.

My aunt never made it to Havana. She never danced to "Lagrimas Negras" under a Cuban moon. She never worked her naturally copper-colored body into a swimsuit to lie out on a beach, not in Havana, Veracruz, or later in Chicago, where she and my mother took all of us children to the Twelfth Street Beach plenty of times during the summers. Neither of them went in to bathe with us splashing, tireless children. They watched from the shore with sandy tacos wrapped in wax paper and hard-boiled eggs and Kool-Aid in a big thermos, all of which we had carried on the very long jaunt from our inner-city flats. Too many unruly kids to pile on a bus might have been their thinking. (Or anything to save a buck, which could have been my mother's motto.)

When she was old enough, maybe fifteen or sixteen, Flora left the kitchen she grew up working in and, soon after arriving in Nuevo Laredo to join her grandparents, married a soldier. After two children and before the age of twenty, she was widowed. She remarried—a Tex-Mex field worker with a pencil-thin mustache and Western boots—and my mother urged her younger sister and the new husband to come up north to Chicago. My aunt had learned to cook a wide range of delicacies, and she had no problem adding to her menu her norteño husband's preferences: flour tortillas, pinto beans, fried potatoes and eggs, and, of course, lots of red meat. Tía Flora was never a woman who liked to argue, so she kept her husband happy. But she did love to dance, which he did not. Unfortunately, the cowboy husband never came around, not even to slow dance to please his wife.

By the seventies, salsa was all the rage. Tía Flora developed an ear for the hot rhythms coming in from New York to Chicago, turning them on low on the radio or tuning in to watch the bands on the Spanish channel on the portable TV she kept in the kitchen to keep up with the popular telenovelas. Not normally the jealous type, my aunt's husband resented the swashbuckling actor, Andrés García, who was a regular on the Spanish soaps.

One time, my aunt vividly recounted to me over one of our savory lunches, her husband had had it with her mooning over the actor. Andrés García not only always got the girl, he even got the wives watching him on TV. My aunt's husband said as much as he walked passed the little TV and finished off his resentment with an actual hard kick to the set. Sparks flew out of the picture tube. He went out the back door, smug and satisfied. My tía Flora stood stunned by the stove, where she had gotten a clear view of it all from a few feet away. Her husband had slammed the door behind him. By the time he got downstairs and went outside, however, if it wasn't for her whistle that gave him just enough warning to get out of the way, the busted television she dropped from the second floor window would have landed right on his head.

That wasn't the story I wanted to share about my livewire tía Flora, although that one was a good one, too. We were friends, confidantes, as I have already mentioned, mostly in the way traditional married women with children had friends—in the kitchen while preparing meals, quick chats on the phone between chores, at family gatherings when others' ears were not close enough to pick up private anecdotes. My aunt was the family woman and I had grown into the career woman of the new generation, symbol of hope for possible true liberation from men's incessant needs and demands.

My mother, from whom no doubt I acquired the somber manner that has so often been misinterpreted as aloofness, was so different from her only sister. I've always been attracted to the gaiety displayed by some extroverts. My aunt brought out the deep, hidden lust for life in me that I am very certain she also had and, for our individual reasons, we usually kept beneath the surface of daily affairs. Over the years, as a grown-up, (unlike with my mamá) it was my aunt who received my stories without judgment—news of the public life that evolved from writing, my ended relationships, my comings and goings. One time, Flora told me that in a conversation my mother had expressed concern that I might or could write about our family. My aunt told me she replied, "I don't care if she writes about me. She'll make me immortal!"

There is another story my tía Flora shared with me during one of those moments stolen from her endless duties to a large family, work, and husband, whom, as I recall, did little else but drink. Before the drink took over, he worked at a factory. After that, I rarely recall him not swaying. He also made a couple of benign passes at me, which I did not mention to my aunt, even after she surprised me one day when we were alone and shared how her husband had said how fine I looked. One day when he was perhaps in his sixties, Flora found her man dropped dead on the linoleum floor.

The account I remember fondly had to do with the super salsera Celia Cruz. This was before the singer exploded into galactic stardom, before the pink wigs when she became a parody of herself (while still putting out hits), and before her right-wing declarations. I'm speaking of the era when la gente could just go to whatever ballroom Celia with a band of salsa kings came to play at and dance their socks off.

My tía's Celia Cruz remembrance was another example of getting the last say with her husband, with whom, she swore after his death, she was passionately in love all their days. All that week the radio had been announcing Celia Cruz's concert coming up on Saturday at Chicago's famous

Aragon Ballroom. The Aragon was situated clear across town from my tía's casita in the barrio. Her husband had only one female performer for whom he would have spit shined his boots and gone to see and that was Lucha Villa, the ranchera singer who, it was my tía's opinion, sounded like a lovesick ewe. Short of Villa's appearances, he was not interested in the crowds, the price of concert tickets, and most of all, acting all a fool on the dance floor.

Flora, though, had no intentions of missing out. It was only a question of how to pull it off. She made a plan. On Saturday, she went about the house doing her chores. Like many working Mexican women who had the custom of wearing the kind of apron that buttoned down the front and had convenient pockets, my tía Flora always wore hers, even to the market. Her favorite mercado, a good mile walk away from her front steps, was stocked with every ingredient a fine cocinera like her might require. When Flora's husband came in that day (he spent his weekends going in and out until late evening when he'd come in with a six-pack to settle in for the night), she said, cheerfully, "I feel like cooking something . . . *rico* tonight. How 'bout it? Care to join me for a late supper?"

If you'd ever tasted her dishes, your eyes would have lit up like her husband's must have at the invitation. Saturday was date night for the two and she said, "Don't wait around for me, Viejo, I've got a few special items I'll have to pick up." She knew her husband well enough, who, indeed, did not wait around and made his way back to the corner tavern to wait until she'd send one of the kids for him to come have his supper.

My tía dashed on her plum-colored lipstick, the only makeup she ever wore (or needed, I would add, having the gift of a flawless complexion and bright dark eyes), and tucked her change purse into her apron pocket. She hurried off to the main intersection. In apron and chanclas, Flora caught a cab right quick that zoomed her across town to the Celia Cruz concert. "Come back for me in an hour," she instructed the cab driver, jumped out, went directly in, and made her way through the crowd until she reached the front of the stage. "Hija, I danced by myself and made eye contact with Celia, and the young men standing around just looked at me, maybe thinking, 'And this loca old woman?' I didn't care, I got to hear my Celia and I was happy."

An hour later she jumped back in the cab and went home. "What happened to the groceries you had gone for?" I asked. "What happened to the special meal you said you would prepare?"

"Egh!" my tía Flora responded with a toss of a hand as if she couldn't have cared less. "I simply said that the market was closed when I got there. I was in a very good mood when he came home that night, if you get my meaning, and in the end, Hija, a man can be satisfied by other ways than food."

My aunt never spoke of herself as beautiful, but she couldn't deny the sexual allure she evoked in men everywhere she went. Allure that came with sly smiles, mean-ingful side-glances, and other subtle gestures of unabashed flirtation. I still remember as a small child witnessing her in action with the butchers making sure she got the best cut of meat.

I hardly ever recall my mother flirting with anyone, not even with my father, who was a ladies' man. But when he was dying of cancer in his midfifties, Mamá became affectionate with him in front of others. He had never been so with her and, although he was weak and spiritually vulnerable, it was apparent he still did not feel comfortable with displays of affection between them.

The time I remember Mamá's flirtations, they were so unabashed, unlike the intrigue I felt when I'd see my aunt in action, who seemed to possess a kind of Golden Era Mexi-can-film-star treasure trove of nonverbal sexual innuendo. My mother's flirtation appalled me. Later, when my father's philandering became known and I had a better sense of sex-uality as a possible outlet for repressed frustrations at life in general, I wished to hell my mother would go out and get laid. She didn't, even after my father's passing. Even as she aged, though, Tía Flora's allure never diminished.

When my aunt was in her seventies, I saw her effort-less ability to attract men. She and I were waiting in line for tickets at the House of Blues on one of those iced-over nights that have given Chicago winters their renown. We were not waiting to see Celia Cruz but, now, Albita, a new generation salsera. My tía dressed, as always, in a modest but smart ensemble, both of us in wool overcoats that reached midcalf. We were in the long line when an attractive white man, the cashmere-coat-downtown-type, came directly toward us. Handing us a pair of tickets, he said, "I just got an emergency call. Enjoy, ladies." As always, my tía was unassuming about the incident and we happily went right into the large hall.

It was early and the crowd was just starting to arrive. Salsa music was playing over the speakers. We were looking around to see where we might situate ourselves, when yet another handsome man approached us—or rather her—again. This gentleman, in suit and tie, was most definitely age appropriate for my aunt. "Would you like to dance?" he asked. ¿Bailamos? With her usual graceful manner, her thick gold hoop earrings catching a glimmer of the light in the dim hall, not looking him directly in the eye (that would have been crass) but with an ever-so-discreet side-glance, she said, "In a while." Después. The caballero gave a slight nod and returned to the bar to wait.

Getting back to the end of the old century when the world was still good and all that Americans had to concern themselves with was the sexual morality of their president, Flora decided to make the journey back to Mexico City. Apparently, she had unfinished business.

Tía Flora's youngest brother who stayed in Mexico City

left no fewer than ten children as his only legacy. They were all waiting at the airport, grown, many married with children, to greet the from-far-away aunt. (Or at least nine of them—the oldest had made his way to the United States.) The nephews and nieces had a week's itinerary all arranged: a visit to the neighborhood of her childhood; a stop at Santa Inés Church where she was baptized, one of the few places of her childhood that remained relatively unchanged except that it was somewhat tilting a little like everything else. (Mexico City was built on swampland by the wandering Aztecs/Mexicas.) Flora and family meandered through charming Xochimilco, a pre-Columbian mini-Venice of canals, and went on a day excursion to the picturesque town of Tepotzotlán. They ate tongue tacos on the street as she did as a girl and dined at an upscale restaurant with "típico" decor along with the tourists.

Above all, what my life-loving aunt wanted to do, however, was go to the Salón Los Angeles. The old ballroom, which opened its doors in the thirties, still featured cabaret shows and a dance floor where you could danzón the night away. In its prime, it was a premier joint for the best bands of danzón music around. "If you don't know El Los Angeles, you don't know México," remained its slogan.

As my mother and her siblings were orphaned and otherwise on their own, necessity forced the young girls to work at a very early age; by fifteen, my mother was full-time at a factory that made cardboard boxes. It was 1942, and, as my aunt remembered it, my mother, along with two other girl cousins, all of whom worked at the same factory, would dress up after work, put on their red lipstick, slip into their best dresses and high-heel dancing shoes, and make their way to the Los Angeles cabaret. Little Flora waited up nights to hear the tales from the older girls about their adventures at the famed ballroom. It wasn't the kind of place where you'd ever meet a serious boyfriend, but a girl could sure dance and forget for a moment that at 7:00 a.m. she'd be back making boxes at the factory.

My aunt recalled the older girls recounting in the shadows of their room while they undressed and readied for sleep how the band leader always dedicated a number to my mother and her cousins: "This one's going out to the carton girls!" ¡Para las cartoneras!

It made the teens feel a little like celebrities.

Still a child then, my aunt didn't get to be one of "las cartoneras" at the Los Angeles. Here was the rub for Flora, who not only missed Havana's heyday before la revolución but, because she married so young, missed everything everywhere. That's what my tía Flora wanted most of all out of her trip to Mexico City: to dance just once at the Los Angeles. So her nieces, anxious to please their beloved aunt who never came to visit and might never come again and, as it turned out, never did, got dressed up and took her to the shady district of la colonia Guerrero where the Los Angeles still put on shows.

The septuagenarian was thrilled watching the cabaret, she said. It was *La Aventurera*, about a cabaret worker. The legendary composer Agustín Lara's famous song may have been the inspiration. Flora's heart palpitated just as if she had been a teenage cartonera seeing the show for the first time. She even got an autograph from one of the stars (I might add, from the picture on the CD cover, a star who was probably performing there back in the days of las cartoneras). After the show, when the ballroom music began and the old-timers went out to dance, a gentleman (not surprisingly) invited her onto the dance floor. Where did that chronic arthritic pain go? she asked herself. It actually seemed to have disappeared since she had stepped off the plane. "Crafty old knees," she decided. "They only hurt when they're not where they want to be!"

It was nearly closing time and as she was leaving, content to have realized a lifelong desire, she saw a woman about her own age dancing alone. "Well, I just put my bag down, went over to her, grabbed her up, and we started dancing together," Tía Flora told me. "She didn't say a word to me, just smiled and let me lead!" My tía laughed. When she laughed, she got a little self-conscious about her dentures and tried to jiggle them to make sure they were on tight. "I guess that old woman was nostalgic about old times too," my aunt ended her account. "Even the old times we never had!" she added, and then laughed again. She shared with me her souvenirs, the signed posters, music, and all the photographs. "I've done it, now," she told me. "My heart will finally rest easy knowing that at least once I got to dance at El Salón Los Angeles. Whoever said you can't go home again?"

Home, in the case of my favorite aunt, was made of not so much the facts but the fiction of her life, the dreams spun in the kitchen she grew up working in, the lovers that might have been, fantasies offered by television infused into a passionate heart—the stuff and stories that gave her life resiliency.

Once, in her silver years, my tía Flora told me over the phone, "It happened for me last night, Hija. Finally."

"What was that?" I asked, curious.

"I finally made love with the son of the Arabs, you know? In the home where I cooked as a girl," she said. "In my dream last night. It all happened in my dream."

Mamá and I (Gainesville, FL; 1995).

Her Last Tortillas

I did not use a knife at the table until I was about seventeen or eighteen years of age and began eating out with friends. Chicago, where I was born and raised, is renowned for its diverse and delectable dining opportunities. But at home, the custom had always been to eat with a fork (or spoon if absolutely necessary, as with soup) and with a tortilla. The tortilla served as bread but also as a utensil. It is an old Mexican custom that is still practiced by people from humble origins. You tear off a couple of pieces as you would with flat bread when eating hummus, let's say. With one piece in hand you push a little food onto the piece held in the other and, scooping it up, eat the whole bite. The palate becomes so used to tasting tortilla along with food that it becomes virtually impossible to sit down to a meal without it.

Until I was nine and she passed away, we lived with my paternal grandmother in her flat. My parents met in Chicago. Abuelita, who may well have been my great-grandmother, I suspect now, so advanced was she in age, introduced my parents. My mother had just migrated to Chicago with two small children. A year later Mamá and Dad were married, and a year after that I was born.

Abuelita arose every day to the task of making flour tortillas. She was from the beautiful state of Guanajuato, where people ate corn tortillas. However, after moving up to "El Norte," my little grandmother took on the preference for the kind made with white flour. My mother, American born, was raised in Mexico City. She always preferred the corn tortilla. But my father, used to Abuelita's homemade flour tortillas, insisted on the flour ones.

Corn tortillas are very good and what I prefer at home today, if only because they are healthier. But the choice sometimes takes willpower. There is hardly an aroma more enticing than waking to the smell of coffee brewing and flour tortillas roasting on a grill. They are good reheated— but freshly made, with melted butter and rolled up, they are to die for.

Mamá went off to work before dawn, taking buses to the factory. My earliest breakfast memories are associated with Abuelita at her red Formica table making tortillas. As a child, my assistance took the form of play. I was given my own ball of dough with which I tried to mimic my grandmother's motions. I made little tortillas, which also went on the hot grill.

Abuelita passed when I was not quite ten. Since Mamá had a job outside the home, on Saturdays, her day off, she prepared the several dozen tortillas which were to last the family throughout the week. This went on until shortly before my mother's death. Unlike with my doting great-grandmother, Mamá had no time for play and was short on patience. She had a lot to do on Saturdays. Before she got a "wringer" washing machine, there was a very long walk to the laundromat, ironing, cleaning linoleum floors, and many other tasks that fell to her. As I grew into a young teen, some of these chores were passed on to me.

Tortilla making was only one reponsibility to be accomplished before we moved on to the next thing. My older siblings were always out on weekends, and both left home not long after high school. Tradition would have held the role of Mamá's helper for the first-born daughter but, since she was gone, I became the daughter who learned to clean, iron, and, yes, make tortillas.

In the long run, this training served me well. Whatever image one has of a feminist at home, I've always taken pride in the upkeep of my house and kitchen.

When my mother's health declined and I was entering my forties, I took on the difficult task of relocating with my son, moving in to her two-flat building, and caring for her for the next two years. Mamá did not want anyone to come in and clean. She did not always feel comfortable with people seeing how feeble she had become with illness. Mamá had a better relationship with her oldest daughter who came to visit regularly and who shared the responsibility with me to take her to doctor's appointments. As a writer, though, it didn't seem I had a "real" job to go to every day. I was expected to take charge of the household.

Shortly before her death, Mamá had little appetite and said she had lost her taste buds. I'd noticed that she'd begun to reminisce a lot about years gone by, foods she prepared in years past, meals that were not necessarily nutritious, especially to a diabetic. Chitlins, pigs' feet, and wiener tacos were now comfort food to my mother. One afternoon, just back from the hospital, she made a request, which she expressed to her eldest daughter. My sister came in to tell me what Mamá needed. "She wants you to cook for her," she said, dryly. Maybe she was confused about my mother's choice. I wasn't known in the family for my cooking. Mamá's first-born daughter had much more practice. Perhaps, Mamá hoped the lessons I had learned under her thumb and at my great-grandmother's knee would produce a meal that would taste like this side of heaven.

I nodded.

My son had had occasion to taste his grandma's home-made flour tortillas and also yearned for them. In my mother's kitchen, I took out the flour, cutting board, and rolling pin—the same one Abuelita once used. The baking powder, Clabber Girl, with the picture of a girl with a bow that I had seen all my life in our pantries. A pinch of salt. A cup of tepid water.

My mother had a lovely singing voice. In my best tone,

I began to hum as I prepared the dough. Mamá in her room resting. Mi'jo waiting for the first waft of tortillas on the comal. Soon, he too would be put to roll out the masa. Soon, she, like my abuelita, would only live in memory. The tradition of la tortilla linking us, past to present, living on and on.

Me in New York (1976).

Peel Me a Girl

My teens were the most uneventful years of my life, but the world around my pubescent self was exploding.

In the sixties, I was but a fleck of lint in the navel of a waking giant, a small-boned girl growing up in a flat smack-dab in the middle of a city that made the national news every evening. White, male talking heads narrated daily clips of Vietnam combat and boys dying, maybe the one from next door; Johnson's War on Poverty was in full throttle with food stamps, Head Start programs, and urban renewal; the Chicago Seven were rock stars; César Chávez fasted for field workers; Jimmy Hoffa was in prison; Bobby and Dr. King were killed in broad daylight and outraged crowds hit the streets with chants and placards. The most famous mayor in Chicago's history, the boss to beat all bosses, put out a no-shenanigans tolerance edict and sent out thousands of police in riot gear and then national guardsmen to deal with antiwar protesters.

From my back porch we saw smoke rise up from tear gas

set off during the Democratic National Convention. The neighborhood I was growing up in had been razed to start building the City of Oz by the twenty-first century. My family was relocated nearby. With blocks of buildings torn down from the back porch, we had a clear view of the gleaming high-rises downtown.

In 1968 I was thirteen and graduated public school as the president of my eighth-grade class. Against my teacher's advice to send me to a good school, my parents thought I should follow my older (half) siblings' footsteps and attend the public high school in our district. It was the same school my dad had gone to before dropping out twenty years earlier. Riots had followed the murder of Martin Luther King Jr. A curfew was enforced after that.

My grammar school was mostly black. I still remember the children—kind, smart, and well behaved—my neighbors and friends, Monica, Clifton, and Annette with her curled bangs and starched dresses. A few went to Jane Addams's Hull House after school, as I did. If our neighborhood hadn't been torn down we would have grown up together. By the time I reached the fourth grade, my last year before the school was destroyed, however, I was taunted, beaten, bullied, and harassed daily by other kids who were not as welcoming of "the little white girl," as I was labeled. The main bully was a boy named Odell. After one of his mean attacks, I was called to the principal's office. Someone had reported the assault, but it was not me. There was no telling what might follow my snitching. A woman waiting in the office eyed me. It was Odell's mother. Neither of my own parents was there. I can only guess that the school called them at their work, but maybe not. Neither parent ever mentioned anything to me.

"She's such a pretty little girl," Odell's mother said. I was nine, but I couldn't see what that had to do with her son's abuse. How was she seeing me? My mother kept my long hair in braids entwined with red ribbons. I always wore gold post earrings and the practical shoes built to last until you outgrew them and homemade dresses below the knee— all emblematic of traditional Mexican girls. As a child, I was still between Spanish and English, speaking mostly Spanish at home.

I knew how to defend myself. I'd given poor Clifton a bloody nose in the school playground for bothering me too much. But Odell was something out of *To Sir, with Love*, with a motorcycle jacket and combat boots in the fourth grade. He waited one day behind the door of the classroom. When I came in he swung the leather jacket with its buckles and studs smack into my face and sent me reeling.

My family, whose experiences were distanced from that of a young girl in a city fraught with turmoil, didn't get it. They didn't want to do anything but go to work at the factory, collect a paycheck, and squeeze a tiny bit of life in on the weekends. My mother, by doing all the housework on Saturday, relaxed on Sundays by visiting her sister and, later, her oldest daughter, who had eloped. With the older half brother drafted and the older half sister married, I helped my mamá clean the flat. She taught me to iron. She did the important items, but it was left to me to press my father's boxers, handkerchiefs, our sheets, and some of our clothes. This was before permanent-press fabric, which later cut the weekly labor time needed by my mamá and me to one day.

During the week, I was the household's errand girl, going up and down Little Italy. By ten years old and throughout my teens, I was paying the bills at the currency exchange, mailing packages at the post office, picking up corn tortillas at a local grocer, dropping off my dad's dress shirts at the cleaners, procuring cigarettes on the sly for an older sibling when one was around, picking up repaired soles from the shoemaker, buying bread from the Italian baker in our neighborhood on Taylor Street, and dropping off prescriptions at the pharmacy. In the evenings during the week, my mother mended what needed to be mended, and she taught me to use her Singer pedal sewing machine.

My father went out on weekends with friends. They put on suits and skinny ties, got in sparkling Cadillacs, and disappeared into the night. I'm not sure where he went on Sundays during the day, but I didn't see him then, either. Sunday evenings my parents went to bed early in order to rise for work on Monday and start a new week. When they fixed their marriage I was fifteen. The weekend routine remained largely the same except that now my father spent time with my mother.

Now and then, Mamá mentioned the young white protesters outside the factory passing out leaflets as the workers flooded out of one shift and the next poured inside. The
pamphlets urged them to join the Communist Party or some
Marxist-Leninist branch and go to meetings about the people's liberation—a liberation for which my mother had little use. One time, one of the pamphleteers got hired and it
was Mamá's duty to train her. At home one evening, as she
warmed up our supper of daily frijoles, tortillas, and made
some other thing (fideo or arroz or maybe neckbones en
chile verde), my mamá shared with a little chuckle how the
trainee had come in with dog flea collars around her ankles.
The girl had a bedbug issue at home and that had been her
unlikely solution. In other words, the idea of these revo-
lutionaries leading any kind of charge was not to be taken
seriously.

Racial tensions were high then. I didn't want to attend a
high school where I would be targeted as I was by Odell. The
irony about not wanting to go to the local public school was
that color and ethnicity were important to me, too, particularly in a white-dominated city. I wasn't white. You had only
to ask what any European-descended individual thought
of me. With my reddish-brown hue, indigenous features,
and dark hair I inherited mostly from my mother, the usual
comment was that I couldn't even be American.

I identified with popular black culture, though, like many
teens of the time. At bedtime, tucked by my pillow was the
transistor I got one Christmas. If I kept the volume up just

enough, right at my ear so that my mother didn't know I had it on, I could listen until I zonked out. Bedtime hours were strict since my parents were up by four or five in the morning. "¡Sopla la luz!" Mamá would call out from her room. Whether it was because they had no electricity in México or because she picked it up from her grandfather who came from the nineteenth-century rural world where candles or gaslights were used, my mother's order was to "blow out the light." WVON was an all-black radio station and, at night, South Side teens tuned in to hear the latest jams until the wee hours when broadcasting went dead.

Herb Kent the Cool Gent on WVON was a natural born fabulist. Every night he gave installments about metaphorical characters, the Wahoo Man, the Gym-Shoe Creeper (with stinky feet), and the little critters that populated his Afro. They were "green, purple, orange," he said, and very soon you knew he was telling the story of the city's current race relations. Herb Kent had the astuteness to make it not only about black and white but also brown—Latinos. He had a smooth voice, Herb did. I imagined a sculpted face like that of Seal or a green-eyed Smokey type but with a big Afro.

While the station played the Temptations or Diana Ross's latest hits—everything from Motown—they gave shout-outs to mostly black high schools. On my own when it came to education, I ended up at a small girls' Catholic school before transferring to a secretarial school. Both schools had mixed ethnic populations and girls from working-class families.

Neither place had any of the exciting events or associations of big schools: no football or basketball heroes, no bands, no boys, no dressing up how you liked. Neither of my schools allowed teased hair or miniskirts, or slacks for that matter, even during the coldest of Chicago winter days.

On weekends I could dress how I wanted. (Well, not really, because then I was regulated by my mother.) Since I started working at fourteen, I made my own money and got away from my mother's Salvation Army finds for me, her home-sewn skirts made of random fabric, the occasional store-bought dress on sale. Instead, I treated myself to a pretty empire-style dress or sling-back shoes with low pointed heels. I didn't wear much makeup, but I applied eyeliner with wings at the ends à la Ronnie from the Ronettes, and I remember there was a time when my crowd thought smudging under-eye cover on your lips to give you a neutral lip color was the height of chic.

When I was fourteen and fifteen I danced at the YMCA Friday night socials to James Brown's "Say It Loud," but by 1970 the city was at a no-turning-back point for Black Power and social change. Not only had a Democratic president been assassinated but his brother, who would have likely run for president and was one of the greatest leaders for black civil rights the country had ever seen, was shot dead in broad daylight. That day everyone was sent home from school and told to lock their doors.

In this atmosphere—with mostly absent parents, an

inner-city girl with inner-city tastes and dance moves, around inner-city boys who'd dropped out of high school and joined the army or were drafted—I came of age. I caught sight of Herb Kent on the TV console in our living room one afternoon, probably during the King riots when the city was again in an uproar. He turned out to be frog eyed and thin as a Popsicle stick. What a shock. But by then I was developing something of an identity, which comes part and parcel with being a teen. That identity was neither black nor white.

Where were *my* people? They were around. Puerto Rican activists were demanding a new high school in their neighborhood, and afterward, Mexican Americans did likewise in theirs. There were protests. I remember taking off from my after-school job to shout "¡Viva la raza!" and raising my fist at city hall until I was hoarse, although I don't remember what exactly we were protesting on that occasion.

Not that we didn't have ample cause. No, not all men had been created equal in the country, and women, despite their right to vote, most certainly were not seen as equal to men. Right after I graduated from high school, I stopped wearing a bra, and a Mexican college boy I dated told me he didn't think a nice girl should go around like that. I always have liked my breasts, even if I found them mostly obtrusive, and I defended my new right to not be forced into constrictive body armor.

That was my assertive self. Another part was struggling, feeling like an outsider. During those years, I would have liked to have a mother to talk with—or a father. Instead, my parents showed little interest in the young woman growing up under their roof, who spent most of her time in her room in the manner of all teenagers, who cried quietly or loudly and either way was ignored.

I began to suffer periods of catatonia. It was clear to me that my mother was aware of this disturbing affliction because her response was to yell at me from the kitchen that if I kept it up she'd lock me up in the psychiatric hospital not far from our neighborhood. This catatonia stayed with me until my midtwenties. I don't remember any episodes after the age of twenty-four. I didn't know why I couldn't talk at times. I just couldn't and wouldn't. When I shut down, you could come at me flailing a medieval spiked ball and my lips wouldn't have parted.

My two high schools had been small and, how I recall it, there were various cliques that were "in." If you were athletic, let's say, that was one way to be admired or at least respected. Of course, if you were very pretty, girls and teachers both liked you. I had my experiences of being both "in" at times and, at others, singled out. At fourteen, my most awkward teen year, I was lanky and felt plain. Previously an active kid, I was now clumsy at sports. By fifteen I started to make an effort to keep up with cool girls.

As a senior I was in the Spanish club, which was mostly native Spanish speaking girls, and I don't think I spent much time with them. Their first language was Spanish and my Spanish was so-so. Instead, I'd started a kind of underground paper about the eminent revolution. I did almost all the writing and illustrations (I think I drew the red-winged woman straddling a conga on Santana's *Abraxas* album cover for my own cover.) I also did the publishing (i.e., xeroxing at my job on the sneak) and distribution (the school). The girls from the Spanish Club gave everyone a title at the end of the year. Mine was "Miss Intelligent."

I had an after-school clique, not necessarily girls from my school—in fact, a few much older. Our hanging out was a Latina version of Iceberg Slim pulp fiction. A digression: Yes, I had read Iceberg Slim by then. I read anything that came across my field of vision. I'd found a box of his paperbacks hidden underneath my parents' bed. What was I doing under my parents' bed? My mother had a habit of hiding things. It might be the packaged cupcake snacks or oranges she kept exclusively for herself to have with her week-old bread sandwiches on her thirty-minute lunch break at the factory. (She said she wasn't hiding them from me but from my older half sibling who notoriously ate everything when he was around.) It might have been my transistor radio if she'd gotten mad and took it away because I had played it at night and kept her up.

My nosiness paid off with the book discovery; I cut school and read them all. I never knew why my father had those books. At home I only saw him reading the daily newspaper. Now that I think of it, maybe he read them on his breaks at the factory and kept them out of sight at home because of their cover illustrations of pimps and sultry streetwalkers. These were stories told of a backstreet lifestyle that Slim had experienced firsthand, in and out of jail. He was an excellent spinner of seedy tales.

When I graduated from high school and took a full-time job in an office downtown, I used to stop in the sundry shop off the lobby in the high-rise for cigarettes. I started smoking that summer because I was eighteen and could do what I wanted. Like Alice Cooper, I loved it, liked it, loved being eighteen. I'd spin the paperback rack for something to read on the bus ride to and from work. The books I found and still have were *Zelda* (about the wife of F. Scott Fitzgerald), *The Other* (a movie based on the novel came out around then), and *The Naked Soul of Iceberg Slim*.

Back to being a high school freshman: I don't know what I'd have done if either of my parents had come home and found me sprawled on the living-room floor surrounded by all the paperbacks apparently viewed by them as hardcore porn. My mother might have threatened me again with the insane asylum. But they never came home unexpectedly from work, ever. They never missed work. They never called home to check in during the day. You were not allowed to call the factory and interrupt their machines and quotas. And when the school eventually reported to my mother (unable to reach her, the nuns actually came on a weekend morning to catch her at home) about my excessive ditching of school, neither did anything about it. It was a Sunday, Mamá's only real rest day, and she couldn't have been happy with the visit. I may have had a catatonic adolescent depression, but my mother didn't like to talk to anybody on principle. My father was sleeping off a hangover.

Mamá wasn't very religious, so the nuns didn't connect with her. The school was my choice, and with my after-school job I paid my own tuition anyway. As an orphan, being made to work as a domestic as a child, Mamá never attended catechism. She said she was Catholic but she couldn't take communion. My mother was an outsider all her life. Maybe she passed this feeling of exclusion from everything on to me the way some parents inadvertently pass on OCD behaviors.

When I wasn't home in a state of antisocial withdrawal, I went to see some girls I knew; the quasi–Iceberg Slim, late-sixties Latina version of our crew is in my mind. They were around nineteen to twenty-one years old for the most part, but there were a few precocious younger girls. One thirteen-year-old became pregnant. She was white and when the mother let the boyfriend stay over, I couldn't help thinking if that were me getting caught having sex, far from inviting the punk to have a sleepover, my mother would have taken me to an abortionist, then locked me up in the psychiatric hospital until I was eighteen. Only God could have helped the kid when she caught up with him. Why my folks were guarding my virginity is hard to say. There was no dowry to be had. In 1968 the pill had barely made its entrance into the world, and until we mastered birth control, sex and getting pregnant for the inexperienced were synonymous. My parents were adamant that nobody birth babies they could not afford. I was lucky my father had agreed to have me.

Memories of those young women I fell in with when I was fourteen abound. There was stunning, slender, dark Puerto Rican Carmen, whose brother, Edgar or Edwin, closer to my age, was in the clique. No cool guy ever paid attention to me when I was fourteen, at least no positive attention. Edgar or Edwin was the epitome of cool. Sleek, silent, and meticulous in a black cashmere coat and polished shoes. One time a tall, sloppy guy who went by Shadow picked me up without warning and slung me over his shoulder, caveman style. On another evening Herc (for Hercules) led me to an abandoned building to make out. I didn't know what else he had done, but two of my friends explained it was "dry humping." Those girls, my age, often ridiculed me for my naïveté as well as for my use of multisyllabic words. One school friend's brother who answered the phone when I called her one time made fun of my deep voice. His spoiled kid sister sounded like a five-year-old. In all kinds of ways, I didn't fit in at fourteen.

On the other hand, the older girls didn't care one way or the other about whether I went with any boys or not. They might offer me a Seagram's and Coke. They sat around drinking while they smoked, blowing sexy rings in the air. I didn't care for any of that. I liked listening to 45s on a portable record player and doing the soulful strut or singing along with new hits like "I Heard It Through the Grapevine" or oldies like "Angel Baby." I did a decent "Hello Stranger," with two of my girls as backup, having a sultry voice at fourteen and all.

One summer evening, I dropped by Carmen's flat. Carmen was in the middle of a fight with her boyfriend, "Moose," a very tall, fair, good-looking Puerto Rican. He was gone when I arrived. Carmen was very upset and I agreed to walk around the block with her.

Just as we reached the bright lights of the neighborhood liquor store, a car pulled up and the enraged boyfriend jumped out. Long legs flung out of the passenger side—a light-colored Italian knit, his reddish wavy hair in place—he charged toward the trembling girl and lifted her in the air like a rag doll, throwing her to the pavement, a crumpled, shaking mess. Carmen wore gold hoop earrings with very tightly curled short-short hair. She looked sharp in capri pants and overall made a nice presentation. Picture the Marvelettes. Here she was humiliated on the street.

I don't know what happened to her or any of the other svelte older girls in that group. By the time I was sixteen, it wouldn't be unfair to say that I outgrew them. I outgrew hanging out in the neighborhood with girls who were hoping for Mr. Right and, when he didn't come along, putting up with what did.

When I turned eighteen, I was fairly savvy regarding Chicago's dance and social scenes open to brown girls with no cars. Public transportation was always available. There were boys with their own rides. I'd say I got around, but then that could be taken another way. As a high school senior I'd go to tardeadas, Sunday afternoon Mexican dances. I was good at cumbias—the cumbias of then, not the all-over-the-place Mexican cumbias of now. Lounges had real bands, like Rufus, playing funk or rock to dance to, but I could only go to those with a false ID.

It was at a church dance (not my church, to be sure) that I won a dance contest to Tina Turner's "Proud Mary." The kicker was that I hadn't even known I was in the contest until we were the only couple left on the dance floor. My friend Chili and I took the trophy that night, which was a bottle of liquor and, I think, ten bucks. He took the alcohol and I kept the money. Chili was older, had been in Vietnam, and had won the contest the year before. A lot was riding on his reputation. I didn't know any of this when he came to the table and took me out to dance for the contest. That was 1971, the year I finished high school. The sixties were over and a new era was beginning. Soon, I'd be out of wigs, fake eyelashes, and smoky panty hose—instead wearing my half brother's khaki fatigue shirt with *Castillo* on the pocket lapel, bell-bottom jeans, and waist-length, straight Cher-like hair. Now that I think of it, I still wear my hair that way.

By college my parents were even less interested in my school life. Our exchanges were primarily when my mother gave me orders to do some task in the house or an errand, or expressed her disapproval of me. Mamá's indigenous heritage came out then with her best mean face and threatening silence. Chicago had a curfew for anyone seventeen and under, but by eighteen, she couldn't forbid me to stay out late. I was finding a place with my generation, but still felt isolated and different.

Mamá was a stoic, dark Mexican Indian woman who preferred to speak Spanish. We lived in a building where the landlords, directly below us, were never truly respectful of my parents or me. They put up all kinds of rules, which my parents went along with: no pets, no music, no "parties," no guests. We weren't allowed to use the front entrance. Nevertheless, Mamá was strictly ordered to wash the front stairs by hand every Saturday morning.

At eighteen I no longer had trouble attracting young men. I could go out with a different kid every night of the week and, in fact, started doing just that. Anytime one wanted to have a relationship with me, I mocked him and pushed him away. Of course, when I found one I liked, he did likewise to me. Within months, I became a troubled young woman in the worst way, inside, where no one could see it. I never had any kind of alcohol or drugs except at parties, and that was if others were all doing it. I liked hippie LSD gatherings or a Jethro Tull concert as much as the next kid of my generation, but I was just as eager to go kick up dust dancing salsa at the Aragon Ballroom on a Saturday night when the Sonora Santanera blew into town. The time the Los Angeles Negros played I went into full-on fangirl paralysis.

Turning eighteen and finishing high school gave me an immediate sense of freedom from my parents and the law that was intoxicating. Before hitting legal age, if I had gotten stopped on the street past the city curfew (10:30 p.m. weekdays and 11:30 p.m. on Fridays and Saturdays), I could be picked up by the cops, and had been, at least on one occasion. Then there were my parents to face. I took up smoking cigarettes that summer, purely as a dare to my mother's authority. I didn't smoke in her house, but the look on Mamá's face the day I asked my dad for a cigarette on the street was worth my minor rebellion. Now, neither could threaten to pummel me privately or publicly, for that matter, if they spotted me talking with a guy. The formidable bar of restrictions was set pretty high, or so I thought. Maybe I only remember it that way so as to excuse my questionable social skills throughout my teens. I never stopped addressing my mother by "usted." Even in my forties, when she was shriveled and dependent on my physical and moral strength to care for her, I continued to address Mamá by the honorific form: your mercy. She called me by "tú," as one does with peers or, in this case, her lesser.

There are a lot of ways a girl could feel like an outsider, even within her own family. Sometimes parents pick favorites. Sometimes it's your place in age in the family, your gender, or maybe you're the light-skinned one. Or sometimes, there's a serious transgression against your very soul. Henceforth, you live on the outside, possibly outside of your own body. It is where the mother, father, or those who are your guardians deliberately neglect or otherwise fail in their love and protection of you. As I write this, the time between my experience and the present is so long that I can't say it overtly affects me anymore. On the other hand, I suspect it isn't a coincidence that I have found it difficult to maintain an intimate relationship for any length of time throughout my entire life.

By nineteen, instead of hanging out on neighborhood street corners, I left Chicago to study in México. In Chicago I was Mexican and, thus, an outsider. But then in México, too, I learned I was an outsider—a pocha, gringuita, Mexican trash, if you will. Migration has exploded in more recent times, but then, people who went up north were traitors or trash, meaning poor. One night I went on a double date with the medical student I was seeing. He made fun of my pocho Spanish around his friends, and I became further self-conscious that I was not Mexican but a despised Yankee. I stopped speaking for the entire evening. No one tried to talk to me, and I am sure they thought I was a stuck-up gringa.

I was looking for the political context to my identity. My new music was the South American drums and flute, Mercedes Sosa and Víctor Jara. People were being annihilated in Latin America by military governments. Castro's revolution had the attention of Latino youth. While I wrote verses, I still hadn't quite decided on a career as a writer. I was thinking about getting a teaching degree. I'd by then decided my body was my own and having a lover or not was my own business.

I hadn't been old enough to go to Woodstock, but there were other music festivals later for my boyfriend and I to drive to in his beat-up Impala.

While the youth of the country had started raging on its campuses and streets, and blacks were waging their own war on racist and prejudicial legislature and social mores, I helped my mother roll her wringer washing machine over to the kitchen sink every Saturday morning to do the family laundry and later hang it on the line on the back porch. During most of my teen years, above all else, while going through the actions required by school, work, or with friends on the phone—the typical things that typical girls did in typical dysfunctional families in a dysfunctional society—I was observing. Taking mental notes.

When I'm asked about training as a writer, I've always said I never took a class, and I never have. I just started writing and it got out of control. At eighteen I left office work and, without support from anyone to do so, I signed up for community college downtown. It's true, I probably would have continued as a file clerk if it hadn't been that the boss suddenly hired a white girl, the daughter of an associate. He didn't need two clerks, so he let me go. English 101 was a degree requirement. At community college the class was taught not by a professor but by a newspaperman who ran it like a journalism course. He assigned essays written to elicit a particular emotion. The professor journalist often held court with a semicircle of young, white, male aspiring writers around him.

When it was my turn to read my assignment to the class, I wrote about a kid from my neighborhood named Ricky. Ricky walked with a gimp. He came from a big family. Something was off about him. He wasn't in school and he wandered about the neighborhood all the time. Sometimes, despite the fact that I wouldn't speak to him, he'd walk alongside me having a one-sided conversation. He was small for his age and always disheveled. One time he got locked up at county jail. The next day he was found hanging by a sheet in his cell. I read the essay and, as I'd hoped, the class was moved by the story of this neglected young man who took his own life.

Community college was set up like my high school in that a bell rang to let you know it was time for class and the second bell said class must begin. The professor gave us orders that upon the second bell the door was closed, and if you showed up after that you were not welcome. The day it was my turn to read my second essay aloud I reached the classroom to see that the door was closed. My heart pounding, I opened it anyway and, taking a chance, peeked in to see if the professor would allow me to attend. It was probably awkward for him to have me flout his military-style rules—or embarrassing, as it should have been, considering this wasn't a graduate seminar at Princeton in 1958 but an inner-city community college, with drug deals going on openly in the lobby between indisputably shady noncollegiate characters and it was a wonder I made it up to class at all. Keeping out a quiet girl who was turning in all her assignments because she arrived a minute late once might be excessive, even for a smug instructor. He put it to the class who, of course, thought it was okay for me to attend.

The essay I read that day was about Teresa, a beautiful, insane lady who wandered my neighborhood when I was a girl, throwing herself at men, all wobbling flesh in a too-small bikini. This time, though, the class didn't get on board. "Ah!" the professor said with a certain satisfaction after my less-than-triumphant performance. "So! She [meaning me] disappointed you!" It wasn't a workshop. There was no way for us to discuss how a sexual woman gets labeled a tramp and, therefore, not worthy of empathy.

Since fifteen when I bloomed I was holding at 36-24-36. Just like my eclectic taste in music, my fashion sense, too, fluctuated. When I wasn't in pseudo-hippie garb at school, I dressed up. Like a very early Selena, the long hair went up in curls, and hot pants and vinyl go-go boots came on. With only a part-time job as a salesgirl, I joined a couple of student organizations. A South American man, Pablo or Pedro, led one of them. He was attractive and cocky and not my type. My type was a sweet guy. When he, let's call him Pablo, introduced himself I brushed him off. He was much older than most students. One day running up the stairs in the hallway between those obnoxious bell rings that left halls and stairwells immediately vacant, he and I collided. Not much was said. He must've tried at first to kiss me. I don't remember anything about those minutes except we struggled in the stairwell and I ended up on the floor beneath him while he groped and tugged at my clothes. While I fought him off he whispered in Spanish in my ear, "A man will pursue a woman a lifetime until he gets her. He'll have her one way or the other." I don't know how it is that I seem to remember he was thirty-six, twice my age. Of course, I did not report the incident. I got away and that was enough. Even if he had succeeded in raping me, it was a time, similar to today, when such crimes were rarely convicted and in the process, the victim was put through further humiliation.

If the expression "she'll have to fight men off" sounds flattering, it wasn't to me. Except for a violation that happened while I was in college and drunk, nearly passed out, I always managed to get away. Statistics have held that most rapes occur with familiars. In the case of the rape, I was out with friends and a professor celebrating my twenty-first birthday. It was a family establishment and the brothers who tended bar thought it was amusing to double up the shots in my fruity cocktails. I was inebriated to the point of throwing up in the bathroom, unable to stand on my own, and the professor offered to give me a ride home. Instead, he took me to his apartment.

They say an arm broken in an accident does not hurt the same as one broken by someone you know. Trust is a tenuous thing. When trust is ripped away something else comes in its place, ugly and usually permanent. As much of a betrayal as a trusted professor violating me while I was drunk could be, it was back when I was newly thirteen and weighing around a hundred pounds that the struggle to maintain my virtue first imprinted itself on my brain and affected my sexuality.

That weekend my parents were out of the house, I presume running errands. An adult male relative was the only other person in the flat. He was eating in the kitchen while I sat on the living-room floor engrossed in the huge, thick King James Bible my father had brought home, with its gilded-edged pages and full-color plates of Renaissance and medieval religious art.

I was pulled into fantastic legacies of *begots* and long-bearded patriarchs whom I envisioned in robes, roaming the white-sanded desert of the land of Jesus long before Jesus, living for and defending a nearby God who sent angels and signs and spoke to some directly. The Old Testament was rated X and ridden with violence. Cain killed his brother. Jacob slept with his daughters. The widow, Judith, decapitated an Assyrian general. In other places, God sent pestilence, opened the earth to swallow people alive, and demanded the slaughter of firstborns. Lot was prepared to give up his virgin daughters to be gang raped so as to spare two male angels from being sodomized. What a fierce earth it was once upon a time and so long ago. I was intrigued and totally absorbed, and I do not doubt that some of that reading served as a basis for my fiction-writing drive years later.

It was then that the adult male relative in the apartment came up behind me suddenly and swept me in the air.

X threw me over his shoulder, just as that gangbanger Shadow would do a year later. I hardly knew Shadow. He never flirted or spoke so much as two words to me. These were not the only times in my life when men picked me up out of the blue, held me high like a ballerina in the air, or tossed me over their shoulders like a sack of potatoes. They never asked permission. I don't know why some men think it's okay to pick up children or women without asking if it's okay. It's a question better left to social anthropologists and, as I write this, I hope it is noticed that I do not attribute this male-dominating behavior to my or any particular culture.

"You see? You can't get away," X taunted as he made his way directly to my bedroom with me in tow, begging to be let down. I wonder if these are the very thoughts that animals have when they catch their prey: *You see? You can't get away*. We'd like to think they only hunt smaller creatures for food to survive, but anyone who has spent time in nature knows there is a sport to it. Sometimes, they enjoy taunting the prey before they finally kill it. I have two splendid ranch dogs, a pair of mixed-breed sisters. When they were young, they teamed up to chase rabbits and caught birds in midair. They mutilated cats. The dogs were well fed. They obviously chased, tortured, killed, and ate animals for pleasure. Pleasure, or was it their nature?

My bedroom was small and cramped. There was no

closet; clothes hung from a rack and in a metal armoire. He tossed me on the lower bunk where I slept and threw his weight on me, all the while acting as if it were a game I was in on but would not win. I felt my size and weight at least half his, but I was having no part of the game. I felt myself crushed and smothered and a little rabbit heart pounding and about to burst out of its chest. I had no hips, no ass, and no breasts at thirteen. I had just been bleeding six months. I fought against the game.

When I gave a course on feminism decades later at MIT, I found a book at the university bookstore in which a British feminist scholar analyzed society's fantasies about women. The author quoted a study that had asked men what the ideal age was of a sexually appealing female. The resounding response was thirteen. Today, kids are much more aware and wiser about such matters than I was lifetimes ago. If my father hid pulp fiction under the bed and Lucy and Desi on TV were made to sleep in pajamas on single beds, if playing doctor with children my age resulted in shyness because Catholicism class convinced us we'd be damned if we went any further, there were countless other reasons why I fought against the game.

In recent times, I heard someplace that because women are not conditioned to be physically aggressive when attacked, we only resist. It is how we lose the struggle. It is why we die. In my case, I'd grown up with bully older siblings and schoolmates, boys and girls. I was not protected by anyone. No one came to my aid. I was a skinny kid, even anemic, but I had learned not to go down.

Groping for the closest object I could grab, my fingers grazed a phone set on the 1940s second-hand dresser. It was just barely within arm's length. I grabbed the receiver and with all my might conked X on the back of the head. He recoiled backward, stunned or unconscious. I made my escape to the bathroom and locked it. The reason I did not run out the door was because he was supposed to be a trusted adult and, while his behavior no longer showed it, it seemed too much for me to go out running into the street. Where might I have gone to anyway? I was in an apartment building in a crowded city, and yet there was nowhere and no one.

More than this was the fact that we could not speak aloud what had just happened. He and I could not say what had almost occurred. We could not state his intention to rape me. It had been presented as a game.

In the seventies, feminist activists would help improve how rape victims were treated, but before then, leaving things unspoken was the usual modus operandi within families and communities. Everyone involved knew it did little, if any, good to report to the authorities. The crime of rape was considered a violation against society. The victim served only as witness. In other words, it was her word against his or theirs. The ordeal of an investigation and a trial, if it came to that, was hard on families. Either way, a girl's life might be ruined and an entire family was torn apart. There was no question in my mind then—and it would be confirmed again years to come when X continued to impose himself on young relatives—that my family was not the reporting type. I was on my own, in that small bathroom with the claw-footed tub and locked door.

A day or so later when my mother was in the kitchen preparing supper after work, heating up the pot of beans and tortillas, adding something else to pep up the meal, I tried to tell her what had happened. She did not stop her tasks. She did not look me in the eye. She had no questions, nor did she even seem surprised. She simply advised, "A man is a man before anything else," as if she had had that line memorized since the time of her own girlhood. I never brought it up again, not when X later spied on me as I dressed in my room or when he tried other things we can justifiably call inappropriate. In the family, it was impossible to avoid him.

Moreover, he was the kind of man that if you even made eye contact he considered it a come-on of some sort. When I think back about myself as a young woman, I used to always lower my head when passing men on the street, avoiding eye contact. It was the era.

By the time Pablo dragged me down to the floor in the college stairwell, I could physically defend myself as I had learned to do on other occasions. While I found it wise not to report the attempted rape, it wasn't from lack of gumption but practical reasoning.

My one experience with the police led me to believe that

they would never have my back. That summer, when I was eighteen, a friend recently discharged from the army and his family moved to a white, middle-class neighborhood lined with individual family homes. My old friend from the days of dancing at YMCA socials came by for me and we took the two or three buses to his family's new home to say hello to everyone. In the early evening, we decided to go to a nearby park to play Frisbee along with his kid sister, who was seventeen. It was summer and I was in cutoff shorts and a halter top. I carried a combination cigarette-change purse.

We, the only Latinos with a few white kids, strolled around the neighborhood. The group was growing on the street, teenagers out on a hot city night, when a cop car came by and stopped. "Get off the street!" an officer called. Another cop got out of the car and began harassing us. He took my change purse, pulled out a tampon I was carrying, and held it up as if trying to figure out what it was. Besides my cigarettes, there was my bus fare and a couple of Darvon capsules. "What are these?" he demanded.

They had been given to me a week before when I was in a car accident with my dad, who had been driving intoxicated after a family get-together. I went through the windshield. (Seatbelts existed, aircraft style, but were not law then.) At the emergency room, after X-rays determined I hadn't cracked my skull, I was given the Darvons for the pain. After a bit more harassment of the others, the cops left us alone.

All those white kids, my friends, and I weren't doing

anything illegal, not even loitering in a public place, since we had assembled on the front steps of one of their homes. It was the era of zero tolerance as far as Daley's attitude was toward groups congregating in public. Youth were harassed all the time. The Black Panthers were getting raided on the South Side, and apparently, even on the North Side in a white neighborhood, authorities did not want to see kids united.

Along with the kid sister and a girl whom I'd just met, we decided to walk together to the corner drugstore still open in the early evening. Maybe we went for cigarettes or soda and chips, but when we came out we were met by a paddy wagon. The squad car had called for backup to round us all up. While we had dispersed and, in fact, the girls and I were on our own, they grabbed and tossed us into the paddy wagon. We went to jail. At the police station, my friend's seventeen-year-old sister was released because she was underage. I was fingerprinted, booked, and put in a big cell with a lot of women I didn't want to know. I didn't see where they took the white girl who had gone to the store with me.

Someone came by and said I could make my call. I phoned my mother. She had little to say and did not ask what in hell I was doing in jail. Mamá called my brother-in-law, but it was early morning before he was able to bail me out. Meanwhile, I was back in the cell with the ladies of the night.

A policewoman called me out of the cell and led me to an empty one. There were open bars, like the kind you always see on TV or in movies. It wasn't hidden away but right there in front of all the activity going on in the police station. She intended to inspect me, she said. She went through my long hair. I had to take off the halter top. There was no bra, and being a slender girl I hadn't much elsewhere to be hiding anything. As I tried to get my halter back on, she told me to remove my shorts. At that point I noticed a couple of male cops that had been walking past return. "Take those off, too," she might have said, or just indicated I was to remove my panties. Standing in the cell, she came up and ran her hand through my crevices. The male cops were still there. The woman officer found the tampon string. That's all I remember. I don't even recall being taken back to the cell with the other women that night, the night before I was told I could leave, but I'm sure I was.

"Try to behave yourself," was all my brother-in-law said to me on the ride home after he bailed me out. He shouldn't talk, I thought, since he had tried how many times to make passes at me until I told his wife. At home, Mamá did not get out of bed when I got in, and I just went to my room to sleep. She never did speak to me about it. Considering how she always tried to lay down the law with her family, I don't know why learning the specifics about a daughter getting arrested didn't arouse her curiosity. Maybe she got the details from my brother-in-law. Maybe it was because I was eighteen and we both knew she had no authority over me anymore.

A few years later, I caught the television news on the

subject of police strip searches on women. It seemed that in addition to what I experienced, a woman driving alone could be made to strip before police when stopped. That these strip searches were being investigated made it seem like they were not for the purpose, or not for the purpose alone, of looking for drugs.

As a young adult the combination of strictness and what felt by then to be a deliberate refusal of closeness from Mamá to me was obvious. My attempts to have open conversations almost always failed. "Why does she want to talk to me about everything?" she said to a relative once in my presence. She did have a close relationship with one of her children. I mention this now only to show that she was capable of it.

At the end of that summer, I'd started the natural progression to adulthood. I lived in the flat with my parents, the same one with no pets, no parties, no guests, and my mother cleaning the front hallway stairs every Saturday morning. My mother had gotten a portable washer and dryer unit and that sped up the household chores a bit. The country was moving toward permanent press by then, anyway.

I spiraled to a dark place by midwinter of that eighteenth year of my young life, the long dark months of winter not the least of them. I had a hard time with men, male teachers, men I was related to, men making passes on the street, men who started off as friends and soon became predators. Of course, I didn't see all men through hostile 3-D glasses.

Feminists came up with the term "sex object" to describe how most men saw most women. My experiences and reflections began to tell me it was true.

In my first year at the community college, I took only prerequisites. I hadn't committed to a major, whether to become a sociologist and save the world one social ill at a time, or become a painter. All the while, I was writing as I had all my life. Free-form poetry with small *i* pronouns was popular then as social protest. It was a good outlet for my youthful rage. I admired Amiri Baraka and Nikki Giovanni, whom I'd discovered. Like its art stores, the city's bookstores—new and used—always had a lure for me. College courses were interesting, even if rudimentary, and I enjoyed learning about anything from the Gregorian chants in Humanities 101 to nutrition in Biology 101.

The real reading, however, came on my own. On the bus, I devoured Hermann Hesse, Kurt Vonnegut, Kafka, and, soon, Toni Morrison and Gabriel García Márquez. My nose was pinned to *The Last Temptation of Christ* in the loud school cafeteria while drug transactions took place, student activists plotted, and newly arrived Americans negotiated with English.

Despite Mamá not having real time, or perhaps even interest in what I thought, I continued to try to speak to her. I'd catch her at her house chores in the evenings or in the kitchen before or after we had supper. I might be put to cleaning the beans or drying dishes as she swept, and I'd attempt to have a meaningful conversation with her, woman to woman.

As I write this, I want to remember us laughing together during those chats. I want to think I gave my mother a little bit of joy with my presence. I know my early paintings caught my parents' attention because I recall receiving a student easel for Christmas when I was seventeen or maybe eighteen. I believe I sold my first painting at a show at that community college. But I don't know that any of my writing, which I started as a child, ever interested her. Designing and sewing appealed to me, and she helped at home but offered no support with regards to the classes I sent myself to at the Art Institute of Chicago. She had another daughter in whom, I think, Mamá invested her own lost dreams, and who was much more like her. Trying to understand why she and I did not ever click, I come to the fact that, in the end, we were different as women. Sometimes, it's as simple as that between mothers and daughters.

In another ten years, it seemed I might have bloomed in my mother's eyes, as she began to see someone in me she admired or liked. In my late twenties, she made comments that led me to think she considered me attractive. And later, after my father died when I was in my midthirties, she vowed to be there for me, and was—for three wonderful years. Then, she fell back to her old self with me. She talked behind my back. She acted as if she didn't understand anything about me, and that made her suspicious of my actions and behavior. It was much like that by the time Mamá passed away. She was very sick and, by then, mostly she just wanted to be cared for by me.

The long winter that followed being eighteen offered only more confusion as to life's meaning. I became depressed. One particular Saturday in midwinter, the walls closed in on me. I felt acutely the vast separation between the world and me that had been building up throughout all my teens. I was alone at home as on most Saturday evenings. My parents would be out until late, so I began to drink a bottle of my father's Scotch. I wasn't a drinker. Neither was my mother, but I remember the day I came home to see Mamá drinking straight from the Cutty Sark bottle when she found out my father had a mistress. So, perhaps, I first took swigs to imitate what my mother had done to ease the shock of life's letdowns.

At some point that Saturday, I called a friend to talk about all that made me so miserable. As a teenager there was no way to know that while there would be many more letdowns, I could and would always overcome them. It wouldn't be that each hardship made me stronger but that, in fact, I was made of what it took to surmount what life threw my way. All one had to see was female lineage: Mamá's example of endurance and her no-nonsense discipline. My abuelita, the medicine woman with no garden, grew healing herbs in coffee cans. She was my caretaker as a child, who had

come to Chicago escaping la revolución and had outlived all
her men and her only daughter. My maternal great-grandmother, Mamá Grande, whom I loved, was still alive then
in México. Mamá Grande had traveled alone up to Chicago
when I was born. (The winters sent her back to México.)
We wrote letters to each other. My tía Flora's cheerfulness
despite one blow after the next—from young widowhood
and, much later, sons who went in and out of jail and, even
later, a grandson who committed suicide.

I came from indigenous people with deep earth connections to North America that no new nation, settlers, invaders, or conquistadors could diminish. I did not realize these
things at eighteen. This history certainly was not taught in
schools. Mamá kept mostly silent about any personal history. In time, I would seek out what ammunition I needed to
defend myself against society's aggressions, but in Chicago
in 1971, only white people's opinions, histories, and culture
seemed to matter.

That Saturday with the bottle of Scotch, I started taking
aspirins like M&Ms. My mother kept a family-size bottle in
the medicine cabinet. I aimed to take it all. My anger and
self-pity grew, and I kept swallowing tablets with the alcohol until I passed out. The friend I'd talked to on the phone
tracked down my family, and at some point they found me
and took me to a hospital. It was so long ago now it may as
well have been another girl I am talking about here. There
was stomach pumping and unsympathetic tending by Fil-

ipino nurses at the county hospital. Most of all, I remember my mamá in the background yelling at me. She wasn't vaguely hysterical at the idea of almost having lost a daughter. She was mad at me for being so stupid. Mexican parents always got mad at you when you got hurt.

The day after the stomach pumping, Mamá came around. It would have been a Sunday. By Monday everybody was back to work. I was in bed recovering when she came into my room and pulled up a chair. She brought a bowl of green grapes. My mother tended to only shop for sales, and if she purchased produce she chose what was on its way out. Later, when she and my father lived alone, they did better for themselves. They bought ice cream for their grandchildren and roasts for Sunday dinners. But it wasn't like that during my growing up.

That day, I was no less depressed than I had been the day before, and made more miserable by the treatment at the hospital and my mother's disapproval of me, when Mamá sat down and began to peel a grape. Peeling grapes and handing one at a time to me she spoke quietly.

Funny, I don't remember what my mother said; if, for example, she finally imparted a cornucopia of divine secrets in an attempt to rescue her daughter from the underworld. She may have come to finally hear what weighed so heavily inside that I had found life intolerable. It was a talk I'd longed for my whole life and, yet, it plays in my mind like a scene in a black-and-white movie with the volume down. Vividly, though, I see Mamá peeling grapes from a bowl on her lap. Her black wavy hair in a slim ray of winter sun shimmers, with zillions of dancing motes all around.

Mi'jo at 16 with me at the theater (Chicago; 1999).

Bowing Out

Whenever Mi'jo wants to come into my bedroom he knocks, of course. It's something he learned how to do at five. But in the last couple of years, before he enters he gives me an Eastern-style bow and says something in Japanese, I think, which I don't understand. I don't even know where he learned it. Maybe TV. You think all your child is picking up from television is how to become a cold-blooded killer and then he comes up with an elegant ritual of respect toward his mother.

I am thinking about this because my only child is now fifteen and he is beginning to separate. At the brink of adolescence I heard the first tear at the seam, but he was still a clumsy duckling returning every day to the fold of his mother's wing. Now he is nearly six feet tall and will start shaving soon.

He's kind of got a girlfriend.

He comes into my room, his single mom's room, usually accompanied by his little dog, Rick. The dog is less certain that it is welcomed into this forbidden domain than his master and hesitates when Mi'jo is invited in. I am usually not in the middle of anything that can't be interrupted, my laptop propped on a pillow or frayed tarot cards out for a little nightly musing or I'm reading or doing all three and listening to a jazz program on Chicago National Public Radio. I am always "decent," which is how a woman who sleeps alone usually dresses for bed. No gratuitous nudity on my own account.

Before you know it my almost grown-up boy is sneaking under my comforter and trying to get the dog to hop in too. (Which it does not do, being that the dog is no fool and understands the hierarchy of command in our household: *do not—if you know what's good for you—jump on the mamasan's bed.*)

We have our little chats then, my almost grown-up son and I, about his grades at school, homework, what money he needs now and for what, or about where each of us is at in our lives on that given day. "Are you in a relationship?" I ask him.

I say that word because I've overheard him use it on the telephone with his best friend. I'm trying to imagine what "relationship" could mean to a pair of fifteen-year-olds.

"I don't know," he says. I guess he's trying to understand what it means to him, too.

"You're too young," I say, predictably to him as the strictest mother he knows. "You're like a green corn. You're not ready to give anything. Too green."

"And you're too old for a relationship," he says, also predictably as a teenager who has to get in the last word. It doesn't have to make any sense as long as it's the last word.

Well, I'm not in any "relationship" so it's a moot point at the moment, but I must admit he's got me there. I'm pretty content dancing solo and, like a bona fide bachelor, getting very accustomed to my habits. (I'd say "bachelorette" but it would call to mind *The Dating Game* show and that's something I really don't do anymore, not to mention the fact that I can recall that program very likely makes Mi'jo's point.) Maybe my wise fifteen-year-old is right, perhaps I have gotten too old for a relationship. If he's too green, possibly you could also get so ripe you need to stand all on your own to be fully appreciated by everyone, no compromises, no fifty-fifty sharing. Most importantly, no shared bathroom. (There are two basins in my bathroom but one is used for a flowerpot.)

But what I say to my son is this: "Go to bed. I pay the bills around here. I can do whatever I want."

"I'm the man of the house," he says. I can't believe my ears. Before I have a chance to react, he adds with a teasing smile, "I'm the man of the house because I'm the only man *in* the house."

"I am the woman of the house," I say.

"And Rick is the dog of the house," he says with a full-fledged grin and puts his head on my shoulder. Suddenly he's not fifteen and ready to soar off into new horizons to escape the nagging, oppressive ball and chain previously known as Mami, but a peaceful, trusting child who (like his mother, and yes, even like the dog, and every other living thing on the planet) is just trying to figure out where he fits to keep everything balanced—and in harmony.

"Goodnight," I say to my son with a kiss on his forehead, now covered with an outbreak of teen acne.

He gets up; the dog scampers out quickly behind him. Mi'jo, at the door, turns around, bows, and bids goodnight with his Japanese phrase. I wish I knew what he is saying. But I've never asked him. It's one of the many new things about him now that are him and that I'm not expected to understand, just let be.

Mi'jo at age 3 (Berlin; 1986).

On Mothers, Lovers,
and Other Rivals

This is not the story about a love affair. It is a story about *the*
love affair. It doesn't tell how it started or all the good stuff
along the way. It is only about its inevitable end. There was
a lot of good stuff, to be sure. For example, I recall the hard-
earned week at a resort in Manzanillo where we spent most
of the time in our room or by the pool and back to our room.
There were piña coladas, "La Bikina" piped in through
speakers, and how I marveled at how blond her hair turned
with the sun and how golden her skin. Long before safe
strap-on orgies were organized in Nevada or we ourselves
had that talk and moseyed into a women's toy shop, we were
making it happen with extremities and imagination. When
we weren't giving each other orgasms, we read all of Galeano
(with the exception of *Open Veins of Latin America*) aloud. It
was a book we each had read before we met—one of the million points of light that first bonded us.

Going on vacation to that place was my idea. When I

was pregnant a few years before we met, I had been following a telenovela that was set there. Living in a Midwestern city, and pregnant in summer with no air conditioning, the resort looked like paradise. When I was in labor, during contractions I'd close my eyes and project my self to that beach. I vowed that if I got through it alive (not an exaggeration when you're in the last stages), I'd go one day. I told her about my promise and that's what we did—went to an agency and booked a week in paradise.

Then there was that Saturday in autumn. When the fog of San Francisco draped the city as night fell, and after making love all afternoon, she began reading *Pentimento* to me. The next morning my lover went out for scones and then made coffee and we read the *San Francisco Chronicle* in bed. We loved the pink pages and combed them for all the things we might want to see and do. I fell in love with Hellman's language and was already in love with Galeano's. To this day, I cannot think of either writer without remembering her and those occasions strewn naked across starched sheets, smeared with each other's scent, and reading in near whispers. I fell in love with Sunday mornings in bed together with the paper, and no one since has taken her place. There was a lot of shared reading, irreverent sex, and, yes, we wrote. It was with the writing, what we both swore was as important as all the rest of it, if not more, where the good stuff went bad.

My toddler spent the weekends with his father. Funny,

it took a separation to get my husband to spend time with either of us. From that loneliness, I went to a relationship where I was anything but—or at least that was what I thought at first. In time, I would finally accept that loneliness was integral to being alive. Nobody makes you feel that way and, likewise, nobody takes it away. But the memories dipped in "good stuff" tell me that, for moments, the loneliness was soothed when I was in her company. My husband, a good provider, nevertheless made little time for his young family, as I've mentioned. As a full-time mother, I remember that Saturday night and the next morning because it was rare to have the chance to do my most favorite things—read, sex, sleep in, repeat. I remember the good stuff the way a kid remembers a day at the circus, as singular and magical—even if after she grows up she knows it was all tricks and invisible wires, it was real enough at the time.

So far in life, I've been truly in love only once with a woman. How it came to be was like a personalized meteorite had plunged from the sky faster than the speed of sound and left a radiating crater in my chest. It felt like a nonstop poem in progress and I couldn't get hold of its meter or rhyme, if, in fact, it held any. Identity, literature, and the G-spot combined in a single fuse. Because of my cynical disposition, I went around suspicious that soon the gilded fuse would be lit and—boom—game over. Such a potent combination in the heart of a young brown woman poet would surely be the death of her. It wasn't because I had fallen in love. It was that part of me had been validated. Validation proved my existence.

What do I mean by validation? It meant that another person recognized how I saw the world and did not judge me as loca. And what I mean by crazy here is not the kind where you'd find yourself in the loony bin or more often now on prescribed drugs. I refer to the crazy that people think you are because you don't agree with the system or how it treats you as a woman—tap-tap like water dripping every waking second and you must be loca because you've set out to challenge it.

That is what being in love is about, after all, being validated. It was my lover, however, who put the match to munitions during our first rendezvous out of town. It is why this love story is about the end, because the end started so near the beginning.

Regarding our getaway, a friend lent us his apartment near the beach in Carmel. I left my toddler in the care of his father and she and I drove to the coast. I want to say it was late spring or early summer, but the sea is always cold in Northern California and the waves often choppy and gray like they were on that occasion. We took pictures of each other along the hostile shore. (I assume we did, but I don't believe I have any.) Every time I think of being on the shore with her there, I remember a story about a young Asian family on vacation in California. As the husband snapped the picture of his wife and child, a monster wave rose from behind and snatched them up to their deaths. I don't know where I heard this story or if I knew it then. Somehow, for whatever reason, when I remembered it I saw myself as that smiling woman holding her child and the next instant disappearing.

I don't recall what we ate, if we stayed in and cooked or had romantic dinners out. I am only certain that we mostly did what newly minted lovers do best, especially away from society's scornful eyes. It was after sex that my beloved told me what would change our course. She was hopelessly in love with someone else. It was a much older woman who was "ostensibly straight" and had refused to come out.

We had been fucking like two starving porn starlets for days and nights. I learned things about my own body that you couldn't find in books. (My copy of *Our Bodies, Ourselves* was worn thin. It had helped me through pregnancy and childbirth. It was the eighties and, of course, there was no Internet. There had been *The Hite Report* in the seventies, which led me to a kind of *I'm OK—You're OK* view about my desires. But there were things you couldn't know from books even if they came with diagrams.) My lover's confession was so incongruous with our heated coupling that I had no way to process the letdown.

The other woman was not at fault for the infliction that began to fester where the meteorite had landed. Apparently, after a tryst that had occurred perhaps two or three years earlier, she'd made her feelings clear. She wanted only to maintain the friendship, which had a basis in their shared radical feminist-of-color views. If literature fed our souls as writers, the content of that literature was the acknowledgment of our perceptions. Our writing made them real. I had nothing but respect for their alliance.

Feminists of color had to be united. The two hadn't been sharing cups of sugar across the fence and one day decided to fuck and see what it was like. In the seventies and eighties, meeting a feminist of color was like meeting someone from the Resistance. These underground liaisons were so vital to the greater cause they sparked all kinds of heretofore forbidden feelings. One held on regardless of personal disappointments. As I saw it, the other woman in my lover's mind had become the "obscure object of desire." In other words, something my lover couldn't have.

Before the extent of information currently available at our fingertips through social media and the Internet, hungry minds learned about life from periodicals, TV, radio, books, and foreign and indie films. Gleaning the kind of information one felt one needed to grow was not easy. In Chicago in my late teens, I caught films at art movie houses. It was where I discovered Bergman, Fellini, and Truffaut. One day, I thought, I'd become a film director and would tell the stories of brown women in the States that no one saw on the big screen. The genre would be called "Chicana Noir" because our narratives were invariably dark.

One of my favorite movies was Buñuel's *That Obscure Object of Desire*. It cleverly related how we (and by we, he meant men) were drawn toward what we saw in a lover and not necessarily what was there. As feminist thought developed, women (as well as most marginalized people) would be referred to as "other." But before that was written out by intelligent and learned feminist minds, as one who was often seen as "exotic," therefore sexualized, I identified with Buñuel's film. To this day, I don't think that most of the men I've ever dealt with intimately knew me. Instead, they saw what they wanted to see.

What I heard from my lover that afternoon when the bubble of what I considered our sublime union had burst was that she wanted that woman to be someone for her that she was not. My head throbbed and ears rang as if I'd just heard a mine explode. ¡Qué barbaridad! Tell me it's not true! I kept thinking. If the political agenda of the radical feminist lesbian was to have a right to her sexuality, then who was she to object to the choices other women made?

It was an era when sexual identity was black and white. There were two genders. There were two sexualities. You were either gay or lesbian or you were straight. You chose one camp or the other. Queer meant being gay and not what it currently refers to now—anything in between gay and hetero. When white women who were identifying as lesbian left that lifestyle to be with men, their friends and former lovers might disapprove, but they slipped comfortably into their place in heterosexual society. Women of color were marginalized no matter what.

I would venture to say that today the other woman might have considered herself queer, not straight, ostensibly or otherwise. But it was a period in modern history of hard-liners. You were either with "us" or against "us," so to speak. My lover declared herself butch and I, with my tight skirts and red lipstick, was classified as femme. These presentations or, as I often call them, costumes, did not necessarily speak to who we were inside. Or at least not to me, as I only speak for myself here. Today, the discussions among activists have evolved such that a wide range of identities may be expressed under the two umbrella terms "butch" and "femme." Furthermore, a person, if she chooses, may change these identities in accordance with the situation. A femme may now identify as femme and be straight. I struggled with wanting to know who my lover was beneath the mullet haircut and trousers. I urged her toward trying other "costumes" and sometimes I took to wearing trousers. After we broke up, she grew her hair out, which I thought softened her appearance. I never knew why she was wearing it long or if there was a connection, but that was when she decided to get pregnant and became a mother.

Somehow I afforded two or three therapy sessions to discuss all this with an objective analyst. I found a Latina lesbian. If she was helpful at all I can't recall, but I don't think so. Mostly, she sat across the room in her office and listened. What I do remember was that having an outsider listen, I thought, was worth it. I was so protective of my lover and concerned that my therapist was among her fans, I never used her name and the therapist found that disturbing. Afterward, I would treat myself to a cup of tea at Athena's Café on Valencia when, with four part-time jobs, my "me time" was over. I had to pick up my child from the sitter and get home to make dinner. After Mi'jo's bath, bedtime story, and lights out, I'd return to work. I had two part-time teaching gigs, but at home I applied myself to freelance English-to-Spanish translations for a textbook company and was also translating *This Bridge Called My Back* into Spanish for a small press. When my husband and I decided to separate, he told my suegra that I was into women. While she agreed initially to let our son and I have the apartment, she said, intolerant of the news that I was lesbian, she wanted me out in six months, which was hardly enough time to change my situation sufficiently to afford an apartment for Mi'jito and myself in San Franciso. It was in large part the reason my lover and I decided to take a place together. We could split expenses.

In the second year of our relationship, we moved in together in a seedy but affordable neighborhood in Oakland. I was miserable there. We made the best of it. During those months we took turns getting Mi'jo to nursery school, after which she returned to write in her study. She had her own writing studio with a door. Since my child needed a room,

I worked in the living room. While there was the occasional random purchase on his behalf, neither my estranged husband nor she paid for his care.

During the months we shared the apartment, I asked her and a long-time friend of mine to act as godmothers in a native ceremony. The friend made a commitment to come around and spend time with my little boy each week, which lasted while we lived in the vicinity. I saw them both as comadres, but no love or care directed at Mi'jo was meant to be an obligation.

Maybe we should have had a sign on the front door: "Feminist Household Under Construction." Everything had to be discussed and figured out. Fairness and equality were paramount. My lover had a type A personality. Dishes had to be done right after a meal, and we took turns with the chore. Toys must be picked up as soon as Mi'jo finished playing with them. She assumed the authority of a parent, often overriding my wishes. All this control became reason for friction between us. One day, as I lined kitchen shelves while Mi'jo played nearby, she came in and gave him an order of some sort.

"Are you my new father?" he asked, trying to keep up.

Questions popped up in Carmel, reverberating off walls, closing in until I said we had to leave and began packing. What was a lesbian feminist doing pining over a straight woman? Why had she encouraged me to leave my husband for her if she was in love with someone else?

It was that day, while passions for each other raged and the potential camaraderie as writers seemed boundless, that the end began. With the confession, it was my lover, not the other woman, who became my rival. When I wasn't surrendering myself to our relationship I was planning my escape. If I couldn't have her, she would never have me. Nora in *A Doll's House* comes to mind now and maybe did then. It wasn't freedom from a man that I sought. It wasn't that I had to prove myself capable as a woman on my own. I was not going to live reflected in someone else's idea of me.

As time went on, her feelings for the other woman, who lived on the East Coast, didn't seem to diminish. A year or so later she pronounced again, pounding her chest and with tears streaming, how she wished the other woman would get out of her heart. It was then that I learned how love could be sometimes. You could utterly abhor (intermittently) the one person you most loved. Whether this was a truth or not, I am certain that was what I felt from the door of our bedroom, watching her cry. In our bed with me so near, she agonized over an unrequited love.

In many ways, the other woman wasn't only irrelevant to our problems, she wasn't real. I felt this despite a framed picture of her that my lover kept on display. For a long time I thought it was her grandmother. When I realized who the hunched woman with bifocals and bun was, it became a good lesson in feminism. Now past the age of the woman in that picture, I am glad to know that real passion has no age or aesthetic limits. In straight relationships, many women suffer the humiliation of being left for younger women. It used to be that cross-generational same-sex couples were not infrequently formed. As same-sex attractions became more acceptable, looks and factors like class and race that applied in straight society crossed over, too, and such couples don't form as much these days. Ageism, however, is alive and well. But back then, what brought same-sex people together was mostly their sexuality, which was so marginalized by society it limited the dating pool.

Drama continued throughout our relationship, which lasted three years. Because we were together nearly every day or at least in touch daily, produced two anthologies, traveled near and far, met each other's families, and lived a public and private life together, those three years felt compressed in intensity times ten. Drama happened all the time, but the farce of the other woman she acted out on an actual stage.

My lover became an actress for her play about the other woman's rejection. She was on the rise. I stood up at the end, clapping enthusiastically and proudly because that was my role. As a writer, I understood that what one took from life was not what was important but the product one created. Afterward, backstage, I brought her flowers. It was a triumphant evening for her and it would have been among the good stuff, but I don't recall her treating me on that occasion like a protégé or her lover but, instead, as among her admirers that night. The loneliness was back.

When I got the courage to leave her, she disappointed me again. Rumors came to my attention that my now former lover led others to think that she had given me everything and breaking off with her had broken her heart. When we met I had been married to a man. Gossip came to me that her supporters claimed my departure meant that I had abandoned the lesbian front. It wasn't that I was more susceptible to chisme than the next person. It was that what I heard rang true of her accusations before we split. There had been fallout all right, which I prefer not to remark further on here.

The fact was, I hadn't left women—I left one woman. Before I moved out of the apartment, she had already replaced me. She'd found a new partner in a position to take her to the next step in her career. In time the city would fete them and I heard the mayor came to one of their openings.

While I have had romantic liaisons with women and, later, men, for most of my life I've remained on my own. During the years that followed our breakup, I was dedicated to producing work, making a living, and raising my son.

During the relationship she had been excited about Mi'jo. We were both in our thirties and questions about motherhood were always present. There was the proverbial biological ticking clock. As women together, however, further challenges were present around adoption: IVF was brand-new and expensive, same-sex marriage was prohibited, partners were not eligible for health benefits or community property. We did discuss adopting a child where she would be the *primary* mother. Since Mi'jo had a father and mother, she expressed feeling left out. Then there was her identity as butch. She asked herself if becoming a mother wouldn't go against being a "masculine-of-center womon." Regarding my child, I had the feeling my kid was a big part of my appeal. (In time, her lament at our breakup seemed to me to be more over the loss of my child than her loss of me.)

This may sound as absurd to young ears today as a time when women couldn't vote, but it was easy then for women to lose custody of their children. A woman who had an adulterous affair could lose her children. A woman who was living with another woman held an additional stigma. If same-sex attraction was yet being reassessed in the *Diagnostic and Statistical Manual of Mental Disorders* used by the American Psychiatric Association, the general view of the public was that it was a perversion. That view found its way into the courts. My estranged husband would very likely have been able to take away Mi'jo, if he chose. This was all a real threat to being a mother to my child at the time.

I fought for custody for her sake, mine, and ours. In the long run, it felt at times that he wanted (or needed) his dad, not just a man in his life or a new father, but *his* father. At the moment, the challenge and struggle to keep my son didn't help the anxiety of all the other challenges she and I were facing as a new couple.

So as not to argue, especially not in the presence of others, I often remained silent when she ordered my child around or insisted he take her hand or sit with her instead of me. My parents came to visit from Chicago and my lover's dominance in the household, especially with their grandchild, chafed. In private, my mother called it to my attention. She wondered, even if we had been married, why would I allow it?

During those months when we shared an apartment, we discussed adopting a child, one for whom my lover would take the role of primary parent. If we split up, she would get custody; as it was assumed, I would have my son.

Soon after that conversation, I was offered a visiting professorship out of town for the next school year. Unable to get work nearby, the job would provide desperately needed income for me. I remember my four-year-old not having a coat that winter in Oakland. His father finally purchased one that looked like he had picked it up on the fly after I had badgered him so much. The vinyl pink girl's jacket he sent stands out in my mind as a symbol of one of the hardest years struggling as a writer and a mother. I vowed that my offspring would never lack for anything and to stop begging his father for support.

Before the lease was up, I moved out. My child went to spend the summer with his father and in the fall, came to live with me to start kindergarten. She and I didn't break up. Her theater career was taking off and she had projects that required her presence. We kept up long distance as we were able for another year and at the end of the second school term we finally called it quits. I moved again to another city to take a new residency in order to support my son and my writing.

Soon after we broke up, she visted Mi'jo and me, insisting she had something akin to custodial rights. On that occasion, when my ex-lover in her usual alpha manner gave him some order in front of me, I'd had enough. As she walked off, I yelled for her to do the world a favor and have a child of her own. Some time after, I would hear she did, but until then, ugly rumors drifted my way that I had taken away "our" son. I think it made a good story for some: the idea that a lesbian activist was being victimized by her ostensibly not lesbian ex. If I sound cynical it is because gossip sometimes does damage.

I'd met someone, too. While we would have numerous trysts over the decades that followed, we usually parted with severe ruptures and never really came together as partners. If the public didn't know about this relationship it wasn't because I scurried back into the closet. My on-and-off-again lover came from a Middle Eastern family with some money; both the culture and her professional ambition kept her attraction to women under wraps. Romantic relationships between women from traditional cultures came with a warning label: "Caution: May produce ill effects and, while uncommon, even death." Eventually, she managed to live her life freely, but that was many years later and with some-one else.

No question, women could mean emotional hell. Every-thing I went to women for in a relationship backfired. Women were indomitably strong in all senses, but they could also be weak. They cheated. They lied. They were vain. Like men who were ambitious, they were egotistical. Some women were chiflada and wanted to be pampered. (This didn't gel with me, unless they were willing to spoil me, too.) Like men, they could fall in love with younger, more successful, or more malleable women. These were the con-clusions I drew from my experiences with both. The good stuff went deep and became integral to my core being. The bad stuff? It helped me grow, too.

Years passed and when my son was in middle school, I had a brief marriage with a man. The rumors from the Bay Area found their way to me again. This heterosexual marriage seemed to be the final vindication for those who thought of me as only having played with a famous lesbian's heart.

In general, I haven't cared much for labels. Sometimes they were important by way of introducing yourself. Many times they were slippery and lacked concision. When you came to the next juncture in your journey, it might call for reassessment and a new description. You weren't recant-ing or flip-flopping when you evolved a label to be true to yourself. We shed old skins, morphed from cocoons, transformed. Even if the outside looks somewhat the same, you never come out the same. The new you is real just as you were real in the previous form. A couple of times I've been identified by the media as polysexual. What is that? I wondered and looked it up. After some thought, I've concluded that it may be accurate.

Perhaps as feminists of color preparing new ground, we were all on unfamiliar territory. It would not be an embellishment to say we went about our public and private lives suited in armor. Our armors were our pragmatic analyses, our evolving theories made from day-to-day living. I'd broken off a leftist straight marriage to love a feminist lesbian without any game plan. We were making it all up as we went along. Neither could say she was 100 percent right and the other, likewise, wasn't wrong by default. *"Who washes dishes?" "We take turns, of course." "Yes, but when?" "Now!" "Now? I don't want to do it now. Don't try to control me." "I'm not trying to control you, but it isn't fair that dirty dishes should sit in the sink while I am trying to concentrate on my work in my room!" "At least you have a door! Close it!"*

It sounds funny now. It wasn't then. Besides the task building of domestic and professional divisions of labor that came up between us as we worked on two books together, I was at times the insecure woman I was brought up to be when in love with a man. To muddle my mind and heart further, my first feminist lover, brilliant and sensitive in so many ways, had issues. As I write this reflection, the matters of the other woman who left her and later, when I left with Mi'jo, to whom she had grown so quickly attached, are not unrelated. It seems perhaps, as I see it now, that fear of abandonment may have been an unexamined issue in her arsenal. If so, perhaps our union had nowhere to go but to end.

A decade later, we encountered each other at a conference banquet. All she wanted to know was how my son was doing, she said. When her current partner left to do something, we got up to dance. The dance turned into a slow one, and in each other's arms, she rested her head against my shoulder. Several people jumped up and began taking photographs of us and the intrusion upset her. "It's okay," I said. "But I give my people everything of me," she lamented. Perhaps she did, I thought with some bitterness. But she hadn't given everything to me, as she told people.

Recently, we had a new exchange. A rumormonger was at it in the worst way and had involved her. To assure me that she was not the source of the poison, she reached out. Nearly thirty years after the start of our affair and despite years of estrangement, there we were on a familiar topic. It was ironic that what brought us together was vile gossip intended to cause animosity. Experiences, like matter, don't disappear. They change form (yes, like identities). Love was an experience. That experience had left us connected. She didn't want Mi'jo and me to feel she would ever want to hurt us. We finished our exchange as proud mothers by sending pictures of our sons, now grown men.

A postscript for you. A couple of years after my lover and I split, the other woman moved to the Bay Area and was teaching at a university. She had included one of my novels in her course and invited me to speak at her class. When the session was over and as the students left, she said, "Ana, I meant to ask you something." At the door, I turned and waited. "Have you ever read Clarice Lispector?" she asked. I had not. Lispector, from Brazil, was from a previous generation and long gone from this strange and wonderful thing we call life.

"Your writing reminds me so much of hers," she said. Walking slowly across the campus, I wondered who the writer she named was who also supposedly came from the same interior world from which I wrote. I went directly to a bookstore. Reading has always been part of the good stuff.

They say there are two sides to every story. This is mine.

Me in Taxco, México (2000).

When I Died in Oaxaca

It was a beautiful day in August of the year of our Lord 2000. I never recorded the exact date so I can't say exactly on which day I died. I heard my traveling companion giving the hotel manager my statistics. She was also my lover. I was lying unresponsive on a hotel bed being attended by two doctors. "Her name is Ana Castillo. She lives in the United States—in Chicago. She is forty-seven years old."

Forty-seven, I thought. What a perfect age. A perfect age for what? you might ask. I might have, too, but I already knew the answer. Instead I asked myself, Where am I? Then I remembered. I was in Playa Huatulco in the state of Oaxaca, one of my favorite regions in all of México, land of my ancestors. I was on vacation. I had arrived the night before. And without any warning, there I was: dying.

Oaxaca, home of the fierce Zapotecs and mysterious Mixtecs, my proud Mexican Indian heritage. Land, too, of the admirable and beautiful matriarchal mestiza Tehuanas and Juchitecas—my kind of women. What a wonderful place to die, I thought.

Cool.

Everything was suddenly, yes, *perfect*. To tell you in the here and now that to find such perfection was liberating would be an understatement. There was and remains, in fact, no way to explain the utterly sublime experience I was surrendering myself to in those moments while I was still conscious enough to hear mi amiga talking to the hotel manager. The closest I have ever come to describing it is in Christian terms (my religious background). It was as if I had found myself in the embrace of God. If you can imagine what it would be like to be cradled and welcomed and loved by a divine presence, this is where I was.

In the meantime, I was aware of the proverbial dark tunnel that I was being drawn into, its soft and distinct low whistle and vacuum pull. This sensation was coming from the right side of my brain. I was completely at ease, voluntarily and gladly "going with the flow."

The left side of my mind's eye, however, was growing irritated by an awareness of what was going on in the room. The two doctors were not inept so much as completely misdiagnosing what was going on with me. That's how people die in the hands of the medical professionals before their time, I thought. That's what was happening to me.

For example, they were sure, without any proper technological evaluation, that I was *not* having some form of stroke or heart attack. But if I had been able to speak I would have let them know that it was, indeed, in the region of my heart that I was feeling an oppressive weight causing an increasing inability to breathe. One doctor thought I was depressed. The other thought I was having an anxiety attack. Hey! I was on vacation. I had just had a swim in the pool and afterward a couple of diluted piña coladas. I had planned to spend the day at a temazcal—a pre-Columbian sauna-type spa—when I was discovered collapsed on a lounge chair. I was well rested. Having had a good night's sleep. I was neither depressed nor anxious as they insisted. And while my working-class background causes me some embarrassment in admitting it, I most certainly was not suffering from overwork.

All the while breathing was becoming more difficult. After two heavy-duty adrenaline shots to each side of my rump—I'd felt my body being turned from one side to the other like a rag doll—I still did not respond.

"Anita," the male doctor asked, testing my coherence, "What is your name?" That was easy. He had just said it just in case it had gotten by me.

"Ana," I breathed out with great effort.

"Who is the president?" he asked next.

This is important, I thought. I really had to let them all know that I knew what was going on. Of course I know who the president is, I said to myself. Then I remembered I was in México. They had just had an election. Who *was* the president there anyway? (This is why you get an advanced degree in Latin American studies, to be able to answer questions like this immediately, when your life is depending on it, I thought.) For some reason it didn't come to me. I had heard the news that morning. Something about the president elect.

I collected all my energy. The really vital point here anyway, I was telling myself, was to let them know that I was in possession of all my senses. It seemed to take every ounce of strength I had, but finally I whispered, "Fox."

I sensed the male doctor's ear close to my lips.

"What did you say?" he asked in a thick Mexico City accent. Again, I was forced to collect myself and barely repeated in the most inaudible of voices, "*Fox.*"

I felt him withdraw quickly and move again to the foot of the bed where I sensed him to be most of the time although I was never able to open my eyes to see him.

"¡No, hombre!" he bellowed. "That's the *incoming* president!"

Great, I thought. So now in addition to thinking I am depressed he thinks I'm stupid.

And that's why I am going to die.

"Don't worry, honey. You're going to be all right," my friend said to me in English.

"Does she drink?" he asked her.

"Yes, she drinks," my friend responded.

I *drink*?

I mean, sure, I drink. But why did this suddenly sound like a crime, proof of a degenerate character and the possible cause of my demise. My friend went on, "Oh, she really socks them away, too! I've seen her. She can really down those bottles of wine . . ."

Oh really? And if I am ever able to get out of this bed, I thought but obviously could not say, I am going to wring someone's neck, not appreciating at all the picture of me that was emerging among the three of them: an over-worked, middle-aged, depressed boozer. Worst of all—in their eyes—single. In México, that alone should have given me reason to want to drink myself to death. (Later, my friend explained that she told the doctor that I drank to prove that the piña coladas at the pool I had just consumed could not possibly have caused that reaction. But instead, the doctors were guessing that I had been doing just that, "socking them away.")

Meanwhile, the female doctor with a gentle bedside manner was squeezing my hand. "Don't worry, Anita," she said in a soft, soothing, but eerily unconvincing voice, "everything's going to be all right. You are going to be all right . . ."

"THE DOCTOR SAYS YOU ARE GOING TO BE ALL RIGHT!" my friend repeated in English to me, loudly from across the room.

"Doesn't she understand Spanish?" the male doctor asked her.

Yes. I wasn't deaf either.

"What? Oh, of course she understands Spanish," my friend answered. I had no idea why she kept repeating everything to me in English. We usually spoke in Spanish to each other. I mean, I may have just suffered the humiliation as a Mexican American of not knowing who the Mexican president was at the hour of my death but that didn't mean my lover had to start treating me like a total gringa.

"Are you sure you two did not have a fight before this happened?" I heard the woman doctor's young voice turn away from me and I knew she was asking my friend.

"No, not at all!" she replied. "We were about to have a day at the spa . . ."

"So you are here staying at the hotel?" the male doctor asked someone. He was asking the female doctor. "Yes," she answered. "I was at the pool sunbathing when the young lady who does first aid came over and called me. She said she didn't even feel a pulse."

Hmmm, I thought. So that's where the time went. I was dead for a while.

"I got some of the workers nearby to carry her up, lounge chair and all, to the room. It was quite a fiasco. They could hardly manage with her . . . We were forced to bring her up in the service elevator."

Yeah, a nice spectacle I'd made too, I was sure, in my Esther Williams flower-print swimsuit, being carried by four lilliputians chuckling among themselves as I began to slip head first out of the lounge chair turned makeshift gurney. While I was aware of the absurdity of all of this but not finding it the least bit amusing, the right side of my brain was directing me toward the inviting dark tunnel.

"Where are you visiting from?" the male doctor asked the female doctor.

"Mexico City. I live in Mexico City but my family is from Tamaulipas."

"Tamaulipas? No kidding? That's where I'm from too!" the doctor exclaimed.

"Where exactly? Do you know the Fulanos?"

"Yes! Yes, I do! We're related to them!"

"No kidding!"

No kidding. Meanwhile, as they went on, a fortuitous meeting of the souls, with so much in common no doubt, I was lying there dying a slow death among strangers. Excuse me, folks, but aren't we forgetting why we're here?—which I believe is *me*—I said to myself. I did my best to muster a frown. Maybe they weren't even looking at me. They went on chatting.

Expressions like how quickly life goes were acquiring new meaning. Suddenly I wished for nothing more than to say goodbye to it properly.

It was precisely then, having that thought, that in the left side of my brain the full-bodied image of sixteen-year-old Mi'jo appeared. He looked sad and confused. Next to him appeared the friend who was back home in Chicago, keeping an eye on my boy. Next to them appeared two of my old-est, closest friends—my childhood friend and my comadre (whose daughter I baptized), both of whom knew that I was on vacation at the time. All four were equally distressed and bewildered. They could not understand why I had left with-out saying goodbye. I had to tell them—I thought—that it was okay. Dying was nothing to be sad about. As useless as lan-guage became regarding such a profound experience, some-how I had to let them know that it was—indescribably—well, sweet.

I, who had thought myself content in life, was now beyond peace and happiness. You see how deficient lan-guage can be?

I felt a tear stream down one side of my face. Then another tear streamed down the other side. If only I could tell my beautiful, sad, confused child that where I had gone was a place of perfection, it would ease his heart. And my friends', too.

By this point my companion had joined in on the con-versation. They all had acquaintances in Tamaulipas. It had become one big happy reunion.

"My brother's wife is from Tamaulipas!" the hotel man-ager chimed in, too. I bet she is, I thought. Don't think someone back home is not going to sue when I'm dead. Sue for what? Who knows? But that's what we stupid gringos do, you know. If I die here in this room you'll all wish you never heard of Tamaulipas.

They went on. Fine, I thought. Life, indeed, went on

without us and I hoped they would all be well. But more than anything at that instant, when time on this earth was so crucial on the one hand and quite irrelevant on the other, all I wanted was to leave a message for my son. I made every effort I could to speak. I put my lips together and in a low whisper I managed to get out in Spanish, "It . . . is . . . very . . . sweet . . . on . . . this . . . side . . ."

I felt my friend get close to my lips, "What did you say?" she asked, with the tone of someone suspicious who had just heard something very disagreeable but still couldn't believe it. Again, I had to fight the weight on my chest and force myself to repeat the words, for my Mi'jo's sake—for those I was leaving behind. I only wanted them not to grieve over my unexplained departure: "It . . . is . . . very . . . sweet . . . on . . . this . . . side . . . ," I repeated.

The room went silent.

And then mi amiga said, "Oh no you don't!" And with an almost simultaneous gesture I felt her hands go under each of my armpits and, with the instinct of a curandera, which we had both inherited from our abuelas (hers, a midwife, had brought her into the world), she yanked my body up from the pillows I was so comfortably letting myself nestle into. She poured the Coke the doctor had recommended down my throat again. I felt the sticky liquid drip down the sides of my mouth. I'd been off of caffeine for two months. I figured I would be having a sugar rush any second but I still couldn't even open my eyes.

I didn't want to come back.

Then I got the urge to go to the bathroom. I felt as if I were coming out of a drugged state, reluctantly returning to inhabit my body. I asked my friend to help me up. I still could not open my eyes. Nevertheless, I heard the doctor pack up his bag.

"Okay, well, she seems to be coming to," he announced. "I am going to prescribe some antidepressants for her. She's obviously very upset about something. So, if she needs to cry, let her cry."

I didn't hear the female doctor leave or the hotel manager, for that matter. Over four hours had passed since my friend had found me in what seemed to be an unconscious state by the pool. I can say without hesitation that until that day, and perhaps still now, I loved my only child more than my own life. But until I experienced what I now understand to be a true blessing, a glimpse into the future, I did not really understand love or life. Love, I learned, transcends this life and life transcends all that we perceive—which means, of course, that both go beyond the limitations of corporeal existence.

Don't get me wrong. I'm not trying to peddle any new-age snake oil here. I do not know even how to end this story and not sound unworthy of your gracious attention. All I can say about the day I died in Oaxaca during a luxury vacation is that I was raised by a woman who never allowed me to feel sorry for myself. Mamá insisted that there wasn't ever anything to cry over—except her death—which is an old Mexican adage from the escuela of hard knocks. Guarda tus lagrimas para cuando yo me muera. (Yo being mi mamá.) So I have always done my best, no matter how down I have felt at times, to remember that things could always be worse. And that, in fact, out in the world, things are worse for a lot of people.

That day in Oaxaca, before the "incident," I had felt content. I was in decent health and feeling good otherwise. Maybe those less than competent doctors saw a depressed divorcée who liked to nip the bottle at midday, but I did not see my life that way at all. I felt loved, truly loved. I was visiting one of my favorite places. Life was good. That morning, over my breakfast of fresh papaya and agua de sandía, I had looked at the day ahead with anticipation and calmness. The pool was inviting and I swam for nearly an hour, an exercise that had become nearly routine that summer. My lover and I were in good humor and had waded out to have our drinks and plan our excursion. Then, without any satisfying medical explanation, I began to die.

In my mind's eye, when I saw the sad and confused expressions on the faces of my beloved son and three of my dearest friends, I needed to tell them that it was okay. It was urgent to tell them that on the other side awaited the divine. Weightless, free, completely connected to everything . . . all of the clichés about near-death experiences we hear on talk shows and read in magazines on airplanes or off best-seller racks (distracted as we always are, one ear tuned out, mulling over why a recent love affair went sour, or how we are going to get ahead at work, that what we really need to shake the blahs is to take a cruise or have a chin tuck), I had just experienced firsthand.

Although I returned home only a few days later, it took me weeks to "come back." I returned to life that day in Oaxaca (albeit, reluctantly) to relay what all of us have heard at some time or another, but nevertheless find very hard to believe, through the fire-and-brimstone legacies of great prophets and the quiet kitchen-table wisdom of humble, God-fearing grandmothers. Simply put: Live well. There's nothing to worry about.

Mi'jo and I on New Year's Eve, Mayor's Event (Chicago; 2000).

Are Hunters Born or Made?

I was in the kitchen one late afternoon during summer when my son stopped by. He was actually moving back home.

The first year of college I put him in a dorm. That sounds as if I had him committed. The truth was, I had suggested in no uncertain terms that he stay in a dorm, and never mind that the university he chose was exactly two blocks from the high school he went to. Both were exactly five quick L train stops away from our place. It was time, his mother felt, for him to take the next step toward independence. His and mine. Just like when I weaned him from the bottle and potty trained him right after his second birthday: Now we do it, Mi'jo. Y ya.

You might say it was always a matter of unilateral decision-making in our family of two. "Such a feminist having to raise a boy!" was the customary response to my status as a mother, as if there were a secret agenda to procreate a race of Amazons. I raised my son much the same way that I would have raised a daughter, conscious not to fall into gender stereotypes. You monitor TV programs, reading materials, music, activities, and playmates. You hope for the best every step of the way.

While he was growing up I began teaching writing residencies around the country. At the end of one school year, and in receipt of a letter inviting me to join the faculty of some department in a university across the country, off we went. Mamá packed, made arrangements, a trail of furnishings and personal belongings left in storage rentals strewn along the way; I sold and bought things as needed. I found new schools, encouraged friendships, signed him up on a basketball team at a Boys Club in one town, sent him off to basketball camp in another (both of which he was somewhat unenthusiastic about, although later hoops became his favorite sport), taught him to ride a bike at five, drive at sixteen, slow dance, shave, do his own laundry from the age of twelve, and once, when he broke my French espresso pot while doing the dinner dishes with an attitude, I made him pay for it then and there. He never broke anything again.

We managed. He grew up; he had about half a foot on me. In high school he lived in his bedroom. He never ate. I was certain that my gaunt, dark (in mood as well as in pallor) child had been bitten by a vampire. Even vampires must learn independence. He took this particular stage with him to the freshman dorm. He didn't care for the dorm that freshman year. He came home to shower. Apparently he didn't like sleeping in the dorm much either: more often than not when I'd get up and walk past his old bedroom, I'd find the blankets on the bed making a much bigger, or more specifically, longer lump than Mi'jo's little Boston terrier, who still slept there, possibly could.

What he really wanted was his own apartment.

"That's why I am putting you through college" was the usual course of our brief exchanges that year. This way—or more precisely, *my* way—someday, with the right credentials, he'd get a job, thereby supporting himself. Then, he could afford his own place.

Nevertheless, the following autumn, at the start of his second year of college, he found a roommate with a job. They got an apartment in a neighborhood I wish I could say wouldn't cause any parent to worry—but that was no different from the neighborhood we had lived in for nearly seven years. Unlike the roommate's mother, who had immediately set herself to redoing the son's vacant room and turning it into a sewing room for herself, I lapsed into a period of domestic confusion. What now?

He'd left behind the bedroom furniture, taking only the bed as well as a spare dresser and futon that had been in the guest room. During the following school year, both my son's former bedroom and the semiplundered guest room remained in a perpetual state of suspension, the absence of any particular accoutrements giving the term "empty nest" literal meaning.

Eventually, even the little dog with its year-round short-

haired shedding had moved out. (Actually, the dog's departure had been at my own insistence. One more opportunity
for my son to learn responsibility, I believed.)

We had been separated many times during Mi'jo's lifetime. Throughout his childhood, his father had maintained
him during all of his vacations and holidays. Sometimes,
agonizing weeks passed during which I received no response
to increasingly anxious phone calls.

But of course, this was different.

Have I mentioned yet that I taught at the same university
my son attended?

With the exception of perhaps one time when he
dropped by, he avoided my office. Fortunately, he did speak
to my colleagues, who would keep me up on his progress. I
knew about his school life during that second year when he
came over that day. It wasn't so much the fact, otherwise. It
seemed that with each rare visit home, he showed increasing signs of intentional disregard for hygiene and other
regimens strictly enforced during his upbringing. And
then there was that one night he ended up in an emergency
room with frostbitten hands. Most grating to a mother or to
any reasonable, mature individual, he continued to refine
his contrariness toward any and all opinions and advice I
offered.

Nineteen, from what I understand about psychological
development, is a critical year for separating oneself from
one's parents. Should I be concerned about just how much

he was rejecting my advice and his upbringing? Even if the answer was yes, what could a parent do when the child was an adult in the eyes of society?

His junior year of college was coming up, and now Mi'jo was moving back home. He could not afford the apartment with his friend. To me, finishing college was paramount and I did not deny the support. I even made it look like it was his idea. That is, once his roommate announced he couldn't keep up with the rent while going to school, I did not have to point out the obvious to Mi'jo, a full-time student. He had a mother living all of a fifteen-minute train ride from campus.

If the truth were known, however, I was starting to get used to my life as a single gal. I liked prancing around in my pantaletas and skinny tees in the morning, among other things single women feel free to do at home when not being mothers. To be sure, I suffered through the same empty-nester syndrome as the next mamá. I did miss Mi'jo. The Good Son, that is the one with the jagged front tooth and traces of baby fat around the middle and Buster Brown haircut, the one with a forgiving nature who never understood why the girl cousin who was exactly his age (as well as size and weight) was so free with the back of her hand. He had not wanted to get into any kind of altercation (which was his father's advice on the telephone) with a girl or anybody.

Growing up, he had been sensitive to others. We had

never taken to yelling at home. (At this writing, however, I recognize that in typical Mexican-mother fashion I lectured a lot.) He learned early on to respect my privacy and my property as I always did with his. For example, he would never have gone in my purse for lunch money. Instead, he would bring the bag to me, as he had been taught, so that I could dole out the dough. He grew up without paramilitary toys. (Prohibition of such gifts notwithstanding, he got a PlayStation on his own and without my permission.)

Overall, Mi'jo was, as I've said, sensitive. Still, I noticed. It happened subtly: my son's definite and undeniable enlistment on the Other Side. Not just becoming a man—a natural process—but one to the fullest extent of the sociological and traditional meaning of gender. A *guy*. How and when it happened exactly I couldn't say. It happened as all things do with young people: with their peers, in their own venues, and by establishing a combination of flat rejection to the standards of the previous generation and enjoying the freedom that came with being newly viewed as an adult. We all enjoy our own language and codes during our youth. We get a kick making the elders shudder at our outrageous rejections of all that they hold sacred or decent, if for no reason but to test our potential future power. With a sense of immortality, we take roof-jumping risks at almost every opportunity. Then, as we grow near the next decade of our lives, it is clear we are not immortal or invincible or even as uncaring about the future and others' opinions as we'd been.

By the time my son was about to start his third year in college and was moving back home, he had definitely become a dude of the highest rank. It may seem to most that it was quite normal for a nineteen-year-old college male to just want sex from girls without entanglements, and maybe it was.

Nevertheless, when that male had issued forth from your own womb, and you had wrapped him in swaddling clothes and waded down the river with him to find a place to raise him away from the Pharisees, a place where he might learn to value the more gentle and nurturing culture of women—where household chores were an equal division of labor, men always put down the toilet seat, brushed their teeth before coming to bed (if not took a shower), and not only listened with marked interest to their companion after the perfunctory question, "How was your day?" but actually cared—that mother did not expect to ever stand in her kitchen and hear the following proclamation: "Oh yeah, no doubt about it. I'm a hunter."

The specifics were the following and I put them to you, the reader, now. As I mentioned earlier: we were in the kitchen when he shared with me how the girl he was "kicking it with" lately had stopped talking to him. We had been away for a weekend, on one of those "family trips," when I had successfully coerced my son to accompany me to an event related to my public life. During this particular weekend he had intentionally not notified the girl of his whereabouts.

"I wasn't that interested in her, I guess," he admitted.

"I thought you said you liked her!" I said, remembering the conversation when he had talked about how beautifully she played cello, the same instrument he played in high school. "You seemed to have something in common, at least." (One couldn't say too much. You mustn't show eagerness to right their world.) I went about my chores in the kitchen. We were going to have lunch—carnitas tacos, one of his favorites. I may have begun to whistle, feigning only the most casual interest in his big, fat, mysterious, juicy life outside the paltry world of my half-abandoned and orderly apartment.

"I like her all right," he said, standing next to me, tall and straight like a poplar tree. He shrugged his bony shoulders. "I just wasn't into her, you know? Once she showed she was interested."

The blood left my brain. Would I faint or grab the nearest blunt instrument at this news that was in such opposition to all the principles I had ever tried to instill in him? Not always by words. Not necessarily by lesson plans. Lest I may be accused of stereotyping all men, I don't recall ever saying outright, "This is what a decent guy does and this is what a jerk does." Still, I held out hope against the monolithic onslaught of society that a mother could get her message across to an impressionable young mind.

Stay calm, I told myself, rubbing the sides of my pulsing temples.

"You getting a headache?" he asked.

"You mean to say," I asked, "that it's all about the thrill of the chase or else you lose interest?"

He nodded. He seemed proud of having elicited that conclusion. In the mid-2000s he stood there, a college boy who loved spraying graffiti on trains with his hip-hop baggy pants and paint-stained hands from nocturnal activities, his T-shirt with photos of Che, Subcomandante Marcos, and Malcolm X with block letters underneath reading: WE ARE NOT A MINORITY. He had political consciousness. He understood race and class issues, especially with regards to Latinos. Nevertheless, I wasn't so sure at that moment that mujeres had made all that much progress from my own days as a young activist in Chicago.

"In other words...," I started slowly, paraphrasing what he'd just confirmed to give myself a little time to absorb it, "if a girl goes after you, you are automatically not interested in her on principle."

"Oh, without a doubt. I'm a hunter." He was smug.

"Okay, Bambi," I said. "As you go off to join the thundering herd, what do you expect from the girl now? You blew her off. You were rude."

People say my son has my eyes. His became very dark at my comments. When he was a child after someone made such an observation, he answered, not quite comprehending genealogy, I guess, or already defiant, "No, I don't. I have my own eyes." Whenever he got pensive, the black raven eyebrow-wings-in-flight soared above the dark eyes.

"I'd still like us to be friends," he said. I couldn't be sure but he sounded a tad remorseful. "I mean, it's awkward when we run into each other now. It would be nice to talk like we used to, at least."

How quickly, I think, we all learn that after that first rush of carnal passion, sex isn't everything. Mi'jo was going on twenty on the autumn solstice; his teenage years were about to disappear behind him, their memory perhaps to plague or cheer him in future, undoubtedly more complex, times.

"So, why don't you talk to her about it?" I asked.

"Whenever I see her, she's with her girlfriends and she ignores me," he said. Perhaps as much as he knew he was a hunter, the girl knew she needed the protection of her pack, I wondered. I seemed to recall years back when I'd been in that position.

"Call her then, Mi'jo," I urged. "Ask her to meet you somewhere for a cup of coffee so that you can explain things. More than anything, women want to be respected as people. Don't pillage."

Pillage?

His eyebrows bunched up. After a minute or so, Mi'jo's slightly slanted eyes brightened. He pulled out his cell phone, went to the living room to call her, and left a message. When he came back in the kitchen, he was all smiles.

We settled down to our lunch, the kind we Mexicans enjoy, especially on Sunday—where you get the meat already cooked at your local carnicería and you put each taco together yourself. A freshly made corn tortilla, chunks of carnitas or barbacoa, add on salsita, sour cream, and avocado slices. It's a cholesterol fest for the arteries, maybe, but nothing beats it. For some reason, both Mi'jo and I insisted on eating standing up, just like at the taco puestos in México.

"You're great, Mom. I'm so glad I talked it over with you," he grinned.

"It's what a mother lives for," I smiled back.

Once he moved back in, I would miss the prancing around in my undies like Jill Clayburgh in *An Unmarried Woman*, a movie I loved when I was figuring things out as a newly minted liberated woman. You could be unmarried, as opposed to divorced, but you could not stop being a mother.

Or maybe you could.

Not me.

Mi'jo and I in the Galápagos (2006).

Swimming with Sharks

Since his father and I split up when our child was still a toddler, I became head of household and both the doting and disciplinarian parent. I've always believed in protecting children from grown-up concerns and never let him know how I managed when I stayed up worrying about bills, when he became asthmatic and we didn't have medical coverage, or, for example, what I thought about the chick his father was screwing around with when we were married.

Mi'jo was thirty when he mentioned the name of the woman himself. I was surprised he knew it. He informed me that when his father had been in town recently he took him to visit his old—let's call her—mistress. I'm sure his dad wanted to show her how the child he took around to her had grown. Back in the days of fincas and hacendados, this was not unusual behavior, the privilege of men with women. We were, however, not only in the twenty-first century but his father had been a communist, not a patrón.

In fact, it was when my ex-husband was—let's just say—

out of town on business for an unusually extended period that my infant son and I went through potty training, bottle weaning, and his first nursery school. We had moved to San Francisco, his hometown. On my own, while he returned to Chicago, I established a life for Mi'jo and me in our new home and location.

After our separation, by taking up teaching creative writing residencies to support us both, I caused a lot of moving. When he was twelve and about to start the seventh grade, we went back to Chicago where I went to take care of my ailing mother. Later, when he graduated from elementary school, I decided to buy him a shiny new bike. The one he learned to ride on in kindergarten was a tiny two-wheeler from the flea market. But several years later, I was able to afford a little better. At the Schwinn bike shop he picked out something snazzy with cruiser handlebars and low wheels.

Mi'jo, mostly a good kid, nevertheless seemed intent on finding ways to undermine my goal to be the perfect single parent. For better or worse, my idea of it included giving him, perhaps not everything he wanted, but everything *I'd* wanted as a kid. The bike was my idea. Perhaps that was why, while I was at the hospital caring for my dying mother, he decided to sell it. Or better put, a kid in his class had offered full price, cold cash.

Mi'jo brought the kid over to show him the bike in the garage. I didn't know about any of this. The enterprising young man didn't buy the bike. Instead, as best as I was able to conclude later, he told some gangbangers about it. We were at home that afternoon when the heist took place. Our small dog's barking in the backyard alerted us. It was a Boston terrier, not a pit bull, so the thieves had no resistance.

It was precisely then, upon discovering that the bike was gone, that Mi'jo told me about the kid and his failed business transaction. I sat down and took a deep breath.

"So, do you want it back?" I asked him.

"Yes," he said.

All my life I'd been sure of one thing about urban survival: once you stood up, you'd best not step down. To be sure, I was trying to raise my son very differently from how I'd grown up. But the world had not changed that much, and in some ways, one had to admit, things had gotten worse. Gangbangers were more aggressive than in my day.

We got in my mint-green, leased Corolla, as nonmenacing a vehicle as one could imagine, nevertheless determined to track down the bike before it got too far. At one point we spotted the enterprising kid from my son's class. He was small for his age, a compact Drake type with a light brown, small Afro. He was sauntering out of the 7-Eleven with a Slurpee half his size and a hot dog. I pulled into the parking lot and we asked about the bike. At first, he knew nothing about it, he said. After a stare down he got sudden recall. He had seen a couple of guys on the main avenue with a bike that looked a lot like my son's. "Yeah, they went thataway."

A couple of years down the line, I'd hear again about this same young man. A horrific event took place in our area that would haunt me for a long time. I first heard about it on the news. A girl in her midteens was having an afternoon birthday celebration. From what I recall, she was from an Eastern European immigrant family, her parents new to English. When the party was ending, the kids spilled out into the alley. One of her guests, a black teenager, was shot by someone. The girl's father and she struggled to carry the young man down the alley toward the hospital that seemed so fortunately near. They reached the emergency doors and ran in for help. They were promptly told by the staff that the injured person had to be brought in; regulations prohibited anyone from going out. While they were conducting this exercise in fruitless protocol, the boy lay outside bleeding and died.

The story was so alarming that President Clinton responded, the hospital was heftily fined, and rules were changed. As a mother, I grieved the unnecessary death of a youth. Some time later, years after my son's college graduation, he mentioned the incident. "Remember that kid who stole my bike?" he asked. "He's the one that shot that kid."

Reluctantly and painfully, I came to accept that Mi'jo lived in a parallel universe from the one we shared within the walls of the condo and from the activities and travels I offered. From the moment he walked out the door until his return, he was a brown male on the streets of Chicago.

All parents, not just in the United States but everywhere, worry that their sons and daughters may not be viewed in public with the humanity with which they are loved and regarded at home. But I've come to be especially sensitive and concerned how males of color, in particular, are viewed.

Mothers have always been accorded much of the credit or blame for making men. Single mothers are held to a special standard since they have "failed" to have a positive male role model in the home. Whether single or married, in a same-sex household or if a mother is completely absent, no matter how well he is looked after, a boy learns from the world. He examines society. He consorts with other males growing up. He learns as much of what it is to be a man outside the home as inside it.

Responding to the relentless onslaught of pigeonholing brown youth (and by brown I refer to many ethnicities besides Latino), Mi'jo developed the proverbial hard shell that we all have to protect ourselves from a hostile environment. Slang punctuated with curse words, a certain posturing, and, whether demonstrated in road rage or on the street, a lack of tolerance of others who took up the space around him began to surface. It made me sad for him.

I found it difficult to accept the anger that accompanied the need for a shell. No privileged education; no birthday cakes and special shopping trips; no visits to Disney World or the Galápagos; no amount of reading at night and culturally relevant children's books; no teaching of simple prayers and humility; no role-model examples of parents, monitoring, and restrictions; no amount of disciplining, I, as a mother, offered could overcome the need for the hardened image a young man might find critical for survival in society.

We may all define survival differently. I've survived economically as a writer for more than four decades. I've survived heartache of all kinds. I survived cancer. I survived the recession and kept the mortgage on my home. I survived years of aloneness in a world unfriendly to a single woman of color. However, I believe for a young brown male on the streets of most cities in the world today survival means nothing short of staying alive.

Back when he was thirteen and on the start of his journey, Mi'jo and I rode in the leased two-door Corolla up and down the main avenue in the middle of five o'clock rush hour. Soon enough, we spotted three guys—older teens, about seventeen or nineteen years of age—taking what looked to be a casual stroll down the street, one pushing the bike along. I made a screeching U-ey and came to a quick stop—just like cops did when I was a teen walking along with my friends—leaving the car double-parked during the thick of traffic, and jumped out. I came at them like Super Mom on adrenaline.

"That's my son's bike," I said, immediately putting my grip on the handlebars. The guy released it. Upon my signal, Mi'jo grabbed the bike, jumped on, and sped off. Now, it was them and me doing a stare down. I said, "Thanks for returning it to us," as if when I ran into them they'd been out looking for its owner instead of a potential buyer.

Something similar would happen to me alone a few years later. Instead of a bike it was our dog. Our Boston terrier disappeared off the porch. People were out and about that warm day. I asked strangers on the street. Someone said they saw the dog with a guy involved in dogfights. My heart pounded when I finally found him in the arms of a young man who turned over the dog without any protest.

"I know how you feel," he said. "I got some pit bulls at home I'd hate to lose."

Our dog was the runaway type. He was so self-satisfied to have his newfound freedom he scarcely acted as if he recognized me. Pulling out a fifty-dollar bill and showing where my apartment was located, I assured the guy and his pals that I would give a reward if they ever happened to find my dog again.

But I wasn't about to offer reward money for the bike.

"I called in the serial number to the police," I lied. "They're out looking for it right now."

"Well," the guy who'd had the bike said, "we found it on the street."

"We're Latin Kings," one of the other guys chimed in. "If someone came by your crib and took that bike, we wouldn't have that."

"Yeah," the first guy said. "We make sure people don't get messed around with." The third guy stayed silent. Latin

Kings as the neighborhood watch. Interesting tactic. What did I know in the midnineties of the Latin Kings in Chicago? Of Latin Kings anywhere or, for that matter, of any gang? The last time I saw a Latin King personally, I was thirteen years old.

I still remember his name. I won't say it. Call it preventative measures. He was a quiet kid. The gentle son of a single mom. One time hanging out, he showed me how to slow dance. Another time he caught up with me on the way home from school. I was in the eighth grade. When we reached my street, I saw the window on our second flat floor go up in a whoosh. My father's Three Flowers pomaded head popped out. He called me by my full name. Then, "GET IN HERE, NOW!" At thirteen I was not allowed to speak to boys who were not related under any circumstances. The boy, the Latin King, was carrying my books. At that moment he not only vanished from the streets but also from my life.

A few years later I heard he was killed. Gang violence due to guns was relatively new then. Such news was shocking. A generation later and henceforth, gun violence has infiltrated American life. The youth seem to be numb to such losses around them. That fact, in and of itself, as I see it, is shocking and tragic.

I also had a brief crossing with the Latin Queens when I was fifteen. Going to socials all over the place to dance with my cool girls, we occasionally ventured into other neighborhoods. We didn't think about territory. We recognized one of the girls from freshman year at our school. She had already dropped out. Linda (I remember her name) approached us in the girls' bathroom surrounded by a bunch of other girls, all Latin Queens. She was light skinned and, maybe to cover up the bad acne, she used thick makeup. Her eyebrows were tweezed to a mere hint of a line. She had gone early chola, with her teased-up hair, dyed pitch black in sharp contrast to pale skin. Back then, gangs wore collegiate sweaters replete with colors and emblems. The Kings' colors were black and gold (or yellow). The girls surrounding us all wore sweaters. Only full-fledged members were allowed this privilege. You wore your sweater proudly and boldly. People could see you coming from a mile away. This was just before guns became the expression of intimidation. Knives were also rarely used. You'd have to come up on someone before they could actually try to rip your sweater off or do you damage if they were in a rival gang. Several might jump you. The intention then was to rip off your sweater, shame you, bloody you, but not kill you. It was a time where life had value and families of gang members were respected. It would have been thought of as psychotic (and I believe it is) to shoot randomly into a crowd, or from a car, or at anyone just because they were perceived rivals. This was before drugs and their associated criminal activities became underground industries throughout the world.

More than likely, my girls and I all teased our hair and wore hairpieces, but not like the way those girls had theirs.

The difference in image was maybe like the singers from the 5th Dimension versus the Shangri-Las.

"You'd better join up with us," the one from our school demanded.

"No, thanks," we said. All we'd gone there for was to dance and maybe meet boys. We eased our way out of the situation. We had to say no with a lot of conviction and, checking out all the exit signs, we slipped out of the hall in the middle of the Temptations' "Cloud Nine," my girl Sylvia doing a mean funky chicken.

Regardless of my naïveté about gangs in the late sixties and generations later, I knew my teens were much more innocent times. Fast forward decades later, three Latin Kings were sizing me up. I stared back. Stares are a Mexican mother's specialty. I stared them down until they were looking at their own shuffling feet.

"Well, I appreciate you looking out for the neighborhood," I said. "And while you guys are on the lookout, I'd further appreciate if you kept an eye out for my boy's safety. I'd hate for anything to happen to him."

The three looked up at me again.

I put on my mamá's best intimidating face. It was the dark Mexican mother's face that seemed to grow darker when you crossed her. Your eyes met and all you could think of was "duck," because whatever she had in reach was going to fly with perfect aim. One of my cousins told me once when we were kids that her mother grabbed a fork off the table and flung it at her across the room. It went twirling in the air and stuck in the door right behind my cousin's face. You had to know her mother missed on purpose, but the point was made. While those nearly grown young men and I had our face-off, I do believe they were having flashbacks of many scenes at home. Or at least, I hoped.

"Don't worry," one finally said.

"Thank you," I replied.

"No problem," another muttered. The silent one gave me a nod. The showdown was over. I got in my car and they strolled off. No one in the neighborhood ever did mess with my boy again.

In retrospect, Mi'jo grew up all too soon. He chose a college in the same city. One day, we were out taking a walk and out of the blue he said, "You've done a good job at raising me," as if it was time to sign off on our unwritten contract. Just like that. He went through school without missing a beat. Becoming an empty nester didn't have to be sad, perhaps, but we needed a way to mark the milestone and to figure out where to go from there. Another day, while we were taking a walk in our neighborhood, I asked him, "How'd you like to go to the Galápagos Islands?" What better way, I figured, to check out the natural order of things?

In his usual cool manner, he simply said, "All right."

The Galápagos, of course, is the famous location where Darwin formed his ideas about natural selection and evolution eventually published in *On the Origin of Species*. As soon as we arrived we felt in our cells we had landed on a piece of the planet as unspoiled as anything on earth. All manner of marine life had adapted to survive there. It was a once-in-a-lifetime experience of glorious boat living for ten days. Once we were standing near a mother sea lion giving suckle to her cub. Mi'jo turned to me as if suddenly our primordial link had clicked, and he poked me in the abdomen, "I came from there, Mamá." And then he asked, "Did you breast-feed me?"

Was he kidding? I considered myself a natural and organic daughter of the seventies and among the last of the great earth mothers. In my mind's eye, I sometimes saw myself as the matriarchal Tejuana with iguanas for sale on her head in Graciela Iturbide's famous photograph. Of course, I had breast-fed him.

The lessons of the Galápagos seemed apparent. Once you came of age, it was your responsibility to provide for the clan. Even the old lizards, crowns sagging, served as lookouts for the young, fertile studs. And speaking of young, fertile males, my strapping young man lost no time in befriending all the women on board. One day, one of the women said to me, "You've raised quite a sensitive son." Socially inept he was not, I had to admit.

After a (great) day of swimming with sea lions and giant tortoises one afternoon, Mi'jo asked, "Why don't you come out with me?" He meant snorkeling. My confidence in my swimming skills had never been great. On the other hand, we'd traveled too far in our handmade ritual for me to back down. It would be a shame to miss out. Plus, I still saw myself as his most important role model. I didn't want to show my own trepidation.

So I joined the snorkelers on their dinghy. Near a cove, the crew guy stopped the motor. He warned us of some strong currents and also the sharks taking a break in a nearby cove. "Don't forget your cameras!" he added cheerfully.

Facing down gangbangers on dry land had been one thing. But facing down sharks would be something totally different. Not wanting to let on I was worried, I had a plan. I discreetly asked an expert swimmer to stay by me in the water.

We all took the plunge. I felt myself being pulled along by the strong currents right toward the shark cove. Soon, I found myself alone and looked around. My surreptitious swimming buddy had trouble with his mask and so returned to the dinghy. Meanwhile, I was carried toward the cove. I began praying when something happened.

Call it Darwinian.

A friendly mammal came to check me out. I felt a long-fingered, strong hand take my small one.

"Come on, Mamá," I heard through his snorkel. He was there, my lanky, long boy. Leading me to the cove. There were sharks and, although not so reassuring, they seemed to be taking a snooze. With a tug of bittersweet relief, I let Mi'jo lead me. We were at a new juncture as mother and son. For the moment, my anxieties about where we'd go from there were put to rest.

Mi'jo just after he was released (2013).

What's in a Nombre

In prison, my son began reading and writing, considering what his life could be once he was released and taking responsibility for the depths to which he'd fallen. I alerted him to an essay contest, for which he drafted the following piece and selected his nom de plume. Renaming oneself is powerful, as is narrating your truths. With his permission, I share his growing empowerment here with you.

My story begins in the early fall of 1983, in a neonatal care unit for premature babies in a northern suburb of Chicago. I was on my way two months early; my mother was taken there in an ambulance. Home-birth plans with a midwife were thrown out. There, with tubes running through my nose, connected to machines, and surviving in an incubator for three weeks like an alien in a science-fiction movie, my mother and father tried to name their newborn son.

My mother's initial plan was to follow Latino tradition and call me a variation of my father's name, the very beautiful and commanding Antonio César. She wanted to call me César Antonio. In all honesty, it would have been fine with me because I couldn't speak up for myself, and that name would have been suitable for a good man, which I would be raised to be. But, stunning my mother, my dad was 100 percent against the name. She did not know that my paternal grandfather, also Antonio César, did not assume his responsibilities with my grandmother, a young single woman. He was married when he got my grandmother pregnant, and stayed with his original family in Ecuador, handing my grandmother a one-way ticket to San Francisco. Nevertheless, she named her son after him.

San Francisco, California, was where the baby, my father, was born and grew up, and one of the cities where I spent parts of my own childhood. Grandmother, herself an orphan, never married; she worked hard and did well in real estate, never returning again to Ecuador.

When my father's father was dying, word was sent to my grandmother. She asked my father if he wanted to travel to South America to meet his father on his deathbed, but the boy refused. The man, his namesake, had never been there for him. What would be the point?

I am thankful that I know my father. Despite my parents' separation when I was three and eventual divorce, I've spent time with him and I've gotten the chance to absorb his socialist politics, work ethic, and honest approach to life. I am genuinely thankful for his existence, and not just because without him I wouldn't exist.

But back to my nombre. As a writer, I have a chance to name myself. In honor of my mother (a living legend in Latino literature), I take the surname Castillo. It is my way of thanking my mother for putting me through college and encouraging me now to write. I add to that Marcello because it sounds refined and reminds me of the cello I played in high school. Castillo sounds elegant with Marcello—like a movie star. Marcello Castillo.

As far back as I can reach into my culturally rich memory banks, I have memories of my mom giving talks, signing her books for readers and colleagues, and carrying herself with grace. In my eyes, she was a powerful woman, like a lioness hunting stealthily among the grasslands for a juicy antelope to take down and feed her cubs. I saw how many hours she spent on the computer revising and proofreading her work, giving birth to the bravest metaphors and capturing ideas that most perfectly represented her people. I witnessed how she was inspired by Mexico and the Southwest, and her impact on Xicana culture.

She wasn't always Ana Castillo. My mother came from very humble origins to create a name for herself. On her driver's license, there is a name equally as beautiful but not as straightforward as Ana Castillo. When Ana first chose her pen name, her mother complained that it was too simple. My mother said that was who she was, simply a person. *Sencilla*. What I came to learn was that this name also protected our privacy—Ana Castillo was a ceremonial headdress, to be taken off at home.

As I matured and was truly confronted as a Latino male in the United States, I began to understand that, despite her successes, my mother had not had it easy. There were people who doubted my mother's work and criticized her because she was a woman of color, but she endured and just kept working and writing. I, too, wanted people to see me beyond the stereotypical assumptions often made. Now, I want to honor my parents with how I live my life. My father, a human rights advocate, and my mother, Ana Castillo, a writer.

Mi'jo playing cello in high school (Chicago; 1999).

Mi'jo's Canon in D Major

It was two weeks before Christmas 2009. At twenty-six, my college-graduated, family-man-with-a-toddler, fully employed Mi'jo committed a senseless robbery. It was crazy. (Was he crazy?) He was unarmed. He could have been shot—killed. I shook at the thought. For those who always blame the mother, who blame all mothers, know that I blamed myself, too. I just never knew for what. Where did the root of the chaos lie?

I watched my son brought into a Chicago courtroom, his wrists in handcuffs and he in an orange jumpsuit. He badly needed a haircut. Spiky hair was growing out and looked like a helmet; he was unshaven, his head hanging. He scarcely seemed present. My only child, la luz de mis ojos, glanced around distractedly. At the time, Illinois had no less than two governors in federal prison. Our country, it seemed, was increasingly familiar with incarceration. And now, we were part of it.

More among us were being removed from society for a

time-out, so to speak, to punish crimes that were somehow drug related and could boost the booming prison industry. Overnight, our loved ones became the charges of taxpayers. We on the outside slept fitfully, knowing that prison wasn't rehabilitation and the penalizing laws that followed an individual labeled "ex-con" made it difficult, almost impossible, to reenter society. When individuals are punished for drug-related crimes, they do not suffer alone. Families, communities, neighborhoods, schools, and political districts all go down with them. Everyone feels alone. The incarcerated counts the hours and days from behind bars, but we are all trapped. Our hearts are broken along with our lives and former expectations.

The morning of Mi'jo's first arraignment, he looked like a stranger to me. The young man I had raised, the boy filled with promise to do fine things in life, was a ward of the state. His eyes were bloodshot. He appeared disoriented—not by his surroundings but in his head. "Disconnected" was the word that came to mind the last few times I'd seen him. He appeared to be strung out on something. *What?* I didn't know.

Cachito, cachito, cachito mio, pedazo de cielo que Dios me dio, I used to sing to my son as a toddler. He knew the words, too. It was a song made popular by Nat King Cole. My parents sang it to me when I was a child. *I look at you and look at you and in the end I bless the luck to be your love*, the lyrics go. The blessing of a child, the inimitable joy of having one, is a little bit of heaven. One of my mother's favorite endearments for me when I was small, and which I later used for my son, was "pedazito de mi alma," little piece of my soul.

That day in the courtroom, I watched a little piece of my soul handcuffed. A piece of my soul looked like society's refuse. His feet were in socks and jail-issued sport slides. When our eyes met, Mi'jo's reddened. *I love you*, he mouthed.

I love you, too, I mouthed back. Quietly, on the bench where I sat, I wept.

DENIAL

From the day I got the shocking news of his arrest to the end of his incarceration, I believe I experienced Elisabeth Kübler-Ross's five stages of grief. According to the theory, they are denial, anger, bargaining, depression, and, finally, acceptance. True to her model, I began this journey in denial. My initial response was so incredulous that my attorney had to send me a video to convince me of my son's crime, after which I went into a kind of shock.

When "it" happened, I was in cold, rainy Padua, Italy, where I had been invited to speak about human rights. Everything went beautifully in that medieval, marvelous town and also in Venice where I spoke at a university. I sent numerous emails to check in with Mi'jo, but they bounced back. He just started a new office job, I reasoned. I tried calling him with Skype but there was no response.

Right before my trip to Italy, I'd stayed the weekend at his apartment. I enjoyed a nice visit with my granddaughter but more than ever, I noticed how my offspring appeared off-kilter. When I last saw him I'd become terribly preoccupied, anxiety nipping at me as I observed his disconnection. He was defensive, unfocused, edgy, and yet inert. I was no psychologist or drug expert but, as any mother would say, I knew my child. Was he on drugs? (This he denied when I asked.) Had he developed some sort of mental disorder, maybe from the inhalation of spray paint? After all, he'd been doing graffiti since high school, I speculated, and asked. He replied by showing me the oxygen mask he used.

On the other hand, he was functioning. It was the height of the recession and before getting laid off from his prior job he had managed to land an even better one. He supported his girlfriend and his child. Maybe it was only me.

In Italy, at San Antonio's Basilica, I lit candles for him at the foot of the sarcophagus of the saint. I anguished the way old-world mothers anguish over their grown sons. I'd seen him through college. He was still my child, my flesh and blood. With no replies to my calls or emails I maintained an outer composure, especially during my public commitments, but inside I was a wreck, worse with each passing day of silence.

The evening when I lit three candles at the basilica—for

my son, his girlfriend, and my granddaughter—the mass was packed. People filled the pews and many moved around from niche to niche during the mass as if it were a small indoor city. After I lit my candles I went to the pew where one of my hostesses had found a place for us. My other hostess, her sister, was restless and left us at the end of the mass.

A very strange thing occurred that evening. I mention it now because I don't know if I experienced it or if I'm influenced by a story the sister who left us told me later that evening. She was quite shaken up after the mass; she said she was going to find a priest. Back home, when we were alone, the young woman told me she believed she had seen the devil moving about the church. What I am not sure about that night is that I might have seen the devil there, too, at the pew when I was with both sisters. For some peculiar reason, I recall a man slipping behind one of the huge columns nearby. I looked down and saw that he had hooves. It was an emotional night, which added to my private worries about my son's mental well-being. Whether or not I had a medieval viewing of a *demone*, I believe it was a sign, if not a projection, of something very negative going on in my son's life. I felt anxious to return to the States.

The long journey home was doubled by almost every holdup imaginable. Unusual security checks of all the passengers delayed the flight out of Paris. A snowstorm kept us in the plane on the tarmac for hours. Once on our way, the crew had to be relieved, and so we went to Boston, an unplanned stop, to change crew while passengers had to stay on board. We finally made it to Atlanta, went through customs at 2:00 a.m., and were all handed hotel vouchers and new connections. The next morning, I joined the throngs of overnight hotel guests fighting to get on the shuttle to Hartsfield. Back on US soil, I kept calling Mi'jo—no response.

It took no less than forty-two hours to finally get inside the door of my own home in New Mexico. I put down my bags and went to the computer to check emails. There it was, the confirmation of my fears and of a mother's instinct—email after email: Mi'jo's girlfriend (who never had emailed me before), my son's father (with whom I had not spoken in about fifteen years), and, perhaps most damning of all, my attorney, who sent a link to a video of my son committing a robbery. It had been on the local news.

A long, dark night alone followed—my own Noche Triste. During the great sixteenth-century conquest of México by Spain, there was an initial victory over the white colonizers. The Spaniards named their defeat the Sad Night. It was the end of a brutal battle in which indigenous warriors defended their nation, land, emperor, and gods. The conquistadors came back, though, and the rest is history. As a mestiza, I empathize with both sides of the horrendous tragedies of La Noche Triste, but never more than when I faced my own night of unimaginable lament, defeat, and hopelessness.

As a Latina single mother raising my son under a patriarchy where wealth and the white race still ruled, I was crushed not to have done better for my brown son. Many parents in this country lose their children every day, some to drugs, prostitution, bad love affairs, overwhelming debts, and dead-end jobs. We lose them when they have their own children before they are prepared to be parents, to cancers and mental illness and to a myriad of other roads that can lead toward devastation. By no means was I unique within my defeat, alone in having an adult child taken into the prison system. But society's entrenched rituals that blame a mother made me feel utterly isolated.

I am every ounce a red-blooded American by birth and tax-paying rights, but I am also the daughter of my ancestors. When a Mexican indigenous mother loses a son, she mourns the loss of a potential warrior by shearing her hair. At the court, when my son looked up at me with his eyes bloodshot from residual drug effects, tears, or both, he, too, saw someone he didn't at first recognize. My hair was cut to the scalp. This is not to say that I had accepted defeat, only that I acknowledged having lost an important battle. I did not lose hope. It was not in my nature.

ANGER

Nine months later, my son was back in court, by then clean and sober. Mi'jo read a letter of apology. It named everyone he had hurt, including the mother of his child, who was present. He was now fully aware of his environment and his situation but there was still something off. As time would progress and he deepened in his sobriety, I'd glimpse the young man I once knew. That day, the judge recognized, perhaps, a good kid.

"I have to sentence you with *some* time," the judge told him, but her compassion was evident, "because you can't just go around breaking the law."

I held my breath.

Yes, he nodded.

"I don't want to see you in the future in my drug court, you understand?"

He nodded again.

I exhaled. I didn't excuse the actions that landed my adult son behind bars—I just wanted to understand them. Depression aside, I was between the first two stages of grief: in denial and *very* angry. Sometimes the stages overlapped, and I could not believe Mi'jo was capable of such a meaningless crime.

Not long before, another Chicago writer had a son who had also committed a senseless robbery that sprung from his addiction. The middle-aged son of the late Mike Royko, a prominent journalist with the *Chicago Sun-Times*, had entered a bank demanding money, claiming he had a bomb strapped to his person. Initially, the younger Royko did not get prison time; he was sent to rehab. The fact that certain individuals—usually white, usually with connections—go to rehab while the hordes go to prison to dry up is a fact of our broken system.

It's not that black and brown communities have an excessive number of weak-willed individuals who have gotten themselves strung out on legal and illegal forms of drugs, including alcohol. People of color are not morally inferior, too weak or dumb to "just say no," as Nancy Reagan advised after her husband, leader of the free world, unleashed a drug war which included flooding poor communities with drugs. We have a broken health system, a mistaken attitude in dealing with disease of all kinds, and no belief that we should provide for our citizens and residents. As a nation and as a culture, we don't believe in compassion for anyone who abuses alcohol or drugs. We have even less sympathy when they resort to criminal behaviors. It is akin to the attitude of much of the public when AIDS was unleashed on the world and the first victims were gay men. The running sentiment in our heterosexist society was that the disease was punishment from God for sodomy and licentious behavior. Disease doesn't work that way. And if you believe in God, I think She doesn't work that way either.

The courts were clogged with drug-related cases. According to a study, 72 percent of criminal cases in Cook County, Chicago, had a related drug charge and 70 percent of them were charged as class 4–felony possession (the lowest-level felony charge).* The details of my son's case were emerging: a few days before the robbery he had been stopped in his car by the police one night, driving with a friend. The officers found a small amount of marijuana and impounded the car. He could well have done something to justify the stop, though if he had that wasn't revealed. Growing up in Chicago as a Latina, however, I knew your brown face could be enough.

Decades before our current anti-immigrant state laws were justifying random stops, a lone cop followed me a good ways before he stopped me with the excuse that a taillight was out in my car. (It was not.) He asked for my identification. Since my late teens in Chicago in the seventies, from my experience with authority—from street cops to immigration officers at the airport—I knew what most likely could get me "off" was not my ID but my fluent English. Once they heard my speech they were satisfied that I wasn't a recent Mexican immigrant, therefore, potentially undocumented. Drug running, apparently, is today a principal motivation of stops—as well as ferreting out the undocumented because their labor is (presumably) a threat to US workers.

The Ferguson riots, the tragic case of Eric Garner dying at the hands of the New York police, twelve-year-old Tamir Rice, and the 101 unarmed black people who were killed by police in 2015 are just a few incidents that pricked the coun-

* The New Jim Crow: Mass Incarceration in the Age of Colorblindness by Michelle Alexander. I will refer to this excellent study here as I have found it timely and revealing on many levels.

try's consciousness about racism. Equally heart wrenching for the public was the death of Trayvon Martin, profiled and shot by a man living in the same gated community as Martin's father. My son was in prison when this occurred. My heart was shattered at the news and I mourned quietly with the boy's parents. A high school student spending a day with his father, about to watch a game on TV, had gone out for some snacks. The release of the young man's predatory murderer reminded our country how cheaply youth of color lose their lives on our streets every day.

Many in law enforcement today, among them brown and black, would bristle to be accused of racism despite the fact that it is arguably often the first rule of thumb when it comes to stop and frisk. Since my son started high school, he was routinely stopped at the train station a couple of blocks from our apartment coming home from school, his backpack frisked, walking down the street with a friend or in a car. "Driving while brown," it's called in Arizona and states where it was illegal to have a license if you were undocumented.

It would be wrong to say that Mi'jo was simply always a victim of racism, but I would have been naive to say that he had not become part of the caste system Michelle Alexander writes so fiercely of in her book, *The New Jim Crow*. While the powerful study focuses on blacks in the United States, she does frequently acknowledge the fact that Latinos, too, are subject to the circumstances she articulates in her investigation about America's drug wars. In terms of color and ethnicity, most Chicanos are mestizos. Some are lighter skinned than others, have straighter hair or light eyes, but the vast majority do not pass for Anglo.

Throughout his twenty-six months of time, mostly in low-security facilities, I reviewed Mi'jo's life, as I had known it, to locate any clue that would explain why my son took the road he had. As a mother, as a single woman, as a proud self-proclaimed Chicana, I had spent over a quarter of a century lighting luminarias just ahead of my boy to lead the way. I strung lights of opportunities to ease the way for this brown person growing up in a postcolonial society. When he was sixteen, he went to see the last of the matriarchal cultures at the Isthmus of Tehuantepec with me. For his college graduation, we sailed along the Galápagos, and he made me proud as he displayed such respect for the women on the trip.

Protect him, yes, with my life; spare him of learning responsibility and to take care of himself, no. During high school Mi'jo had been made to keep a part-time job to take up any idle time and to learn the meaning of an earned dollar. There weren't video games or excessive television time. There were chores and house rules to be kept.

During his teens in Chicago, we lived in a changing neighborhood. I worried for his safety all the time. I often worried for my own. But I held the conviction that my son would not fall prey to gang life or illicit behaviors. At home, he was taught right from wrong.

With the exception of being picked up for spray painting graffiti as a kid (while playing cello by the day and keeping up with grades), Mi'jo had never been in trouble. He never raised his voice to me. I had brought him up since he was a toddler without his father's active participation. His father lived in another state, was dedicated to a new family, and sent no child support, but Mi'jo spent his school vacations with him. The rest of the year, if my son did not call his father, his father also did not seek him out, having taken the approach that it was equally the boy's responsibility to stay in touch.

Mi'jo never failed a class or got suspended. At seventeen, my son asked if he could get a tattoo. I said no. He didn't get one then or later. He never pierced an ear, brow, or lip. Even his diet didn't show telltale signs of something awry. He left some of the healthy eating habits with which he was raised during high school and college but went back to them in his twenties. He took a professional job. Things looked good on paper, as the expression goes. In real life, perhaps not so much.

After graduating college with a double major, he was undecided not just about graduate school but about life in general. He met a girl at a concert. Apparently, she wasn't doing much either. This was his first adult love and they decided to have a baby. My son got a full-time job. As much as possible, I went to help with my granddaughter and namesake.

My son and his girlfriend grew up liking graffiti, hip-hop culture, and, apparently, weed. This is my opinion and only in retrospect; I never saw them smoke. But as my son moved into his twenties, I did perceive him with each visit spiraling into a funk. Despite all pretension to be sociable, I felt an anger seething beneath the young man's surface. I guessed substance abuse, perhaps meant for coping, was at least in part to blame. By his baby's first birthday, Mi'jo was visibly depressed.

He felt the pressure of being the principal provider. He was disappointed in his girlfriend's lack of drive and professional goals. When he said he wanted to leave her, she said she'd keep their child from him. As I was told, she'd threatened to kill herself. Ultimately, Mi'jo decided to stay and watch over his young family. He'd stay until his daughter turned eighteen. He'd figure it out, apparently while wallowing in all kinds of resentments. He was combative, with chips on both shoulders, angry all the time. Try as I did, I could not break through the wall he had built around him.

He'd gone through high school and college almost effortlessly. Behind the scenes, however, was the ever-growing presence of hip-hop culture outweighing personal ambition. When he was a teenager, I packed up cans of spray paint and threw them out—not in the trash bin in the alley behind our inner-city apartment; I drove away to toss them. He said nothing, not a peep of protest. New ones cropped up, one by one, filling his closet and the trunk of his beater. He never argued when I objected to his illegal hobby. He did not talk back when I reprimanded him all the way home from the police station when he was picked up for graffiti. He just kept doing it, well into his twenties. Hip-hop, as he explained to me after his incarceration, was the culture that understood him, his rejection of conservative values, racism, art in museums, the corporate world, and institutionalized religion. As a poet and artist I was no stranger to protesting the mainstream. My problem wasn't hip-hop but how I saw him slipping away from caring about life. And there was the weed—evident in the smell of his clothes, reddened eyes, lethargy, erratic driving, but above all, as time went on, in the diminishing of his spirit.

For the record, I am not morally against marijuana. When my son was in college, I took him to Amsterdam. There were countless young people who traveled there as if it were a mecca for potheads. The place was inundated with homeless kids, like the pigeons in the Piazza San Marco, who'd migrated and stayed, existing for the next high; many ended up sleeping on the streets, bewildered and besieged by drug abuse. Around that period I saw similar tragic phenomena in Granada, Spain. There but for the grace of God I go, I thought, imagining the anguish of parents around the world whose half-grown children were scattered on those streets, their sole purpose to be stoned. One could make a case that I condoned marijuana smoking by taking Mi'jo to a country where it was legal, but he also got to see what abusing marijuana could do.

In the early eighties, around when my child was born, Reagan declared a war on drugs. According to *The New Jim Crow*, Reagan's war, in fact, brought drugs into the country. Afterward, law enforcement was sent to search for drug dealers and abusers and punish them. All levels of law enforcement were rewarded for whatever booty and captured prisoners they might snare. They were given grants, trained dogs, and a waiver on the Fourth Amendment. Media images sprawled across the land warning of black "crack hos" and gold-toothed "illegals" pushing their deadly wares, threatening the total moral and economic collapse of the kingdom. All "decent" people stood behind Reagan's decree. When he went away, they stood with the next and the following, as all successors thought the decree right and just. And by then, the people were at war, supposedly about drugs.

One morning when Mi'jo was in his late teens, I went to his room to wake him and found his face badly beaten. He didn't want to talk about it. Eventually, he revealed that cops had stopped him randomly by the train stop and he had tried to run because he had a joint on him. When they caught up to him, they beat him up then let him go. There was nothing for me to do. Call the cops? Hire an attorney? They would have said he had resisted arrest. They might look for him later.

During his late teens Mi'jo slept a lot and didn't take

meals at home. I kept the refrigerator stocked and prepared food for him that went cold on the stove. (I called him vampire and wolf boy as a joke, but it wasn't funny.) When he came in at night by curfew he went straight to his room. He didn't have a cell phone in high school. He could use the wireless house phone to talk privately to friends but was loud on the phone so I often heard him. He became animated, as he never did around me. He cussed and had a lot of opinions and seemed to have a full life outside our apartment, which could be so quiet it seemed time stood still. I did not blame hip-hop for the estrangement. The chasm between us, whether generational or about mothers and sons or sons and absent fathers, was something many parents endured. We would get through it. I didn't notice (or perhaps didn't want to) his getting high as a teen, but I wasn't blind to the brooding.

As a senior in high school, depression began to rear its ugly and destructive head. His high school counselor called me for an intervention. He might only have been going through a case of senioritis, but when a kid cut classes or stopped trying to pass exams, his teachers and advisors wanted to make sure he didn't slip away—not after all the hard work and being accepted at the university of his choice, they said. When I questioned my son's lack of career goals, the counselor said that boys bloomed later than girls. He himself hadn't decided on a career until graduate school.

Later I took Mi'jo to lunch at a family-owned Thai restaurant. It belonged to one of my son's best friends,

David, who was about to graduate with him. The boys had both decided on the same university in Chicago. Regarding my son's current mood, I offered to send him to a therapist or go for family counseling. Although he never spoke of it, at least not to me, I knew the absence of his father who never called or flew in for a visit caused him sadness. He didn't have maternal grandparents anymore: my father died when he was six and my mother passed a few years later. The cliché that all Latinos come from big extended families isn't necessarily true. I'd been long conflicted about religion, so there was no church support. I suspected acting as mother, father, grandparent, aunt, uncle, and sibling—a village of one—was not always enough.

At lunch, I called in literary recruitment from one of my favorite poets. Not so long ago, I heard the spoken-word performer Lemon Andersen say how poetry had saved him. Perhaps poetry had once saved me, as well. I read my son one of my favorite poems by Pablo Neruda, the one that had inspired me as a young writer to care about the world. "Do Not Ask Me" goes, in part, like this:

> We were born on this planet
> and we must arrange man's society
> because we are neither birds nor dogs.

My son listened without saying much. We had our pad thai and we went on with our lives with or without poetry.

A few years later I remember reading something else to

him that had brought me comfort during one of life's crises. It was after our apartment had been robbed. It was a job committed by a con artist posing as a human rights activist. We were both on the couch and I shared a passage from the New American Bible addressing the recklessness of the wicked who hold no moral regard for their victims. My son was not into reading the Bible but he rested his head on my shoulder and listened.

"In Wisdom 2 they speak: 'Come then, let us enjoy the good things of today, let us use created things with the zest of youth. Let us lay traps for the upright man, since he annoys us and opposes our way of life, reproaches us for our sins against the law.'"

Whether Mi'jo found the words of the Book of Wisdom reassuring or found that in the sound of his mother's voice, with the warm afternoon sun of May reaching us both on the couch, I remember that moment, his head on my shoulder and everything in our world safe again. Evil was at bay.

As I write this, recollections involving the police and other young men my son once knew come to mind, young men of color who ended up not as lucky as he. Not long before my son was arrested, he asked if I remembered such and such a guy from our old neighborhood. No, I didn't think so, I said. Why? "Oh," he said, casually. "The cops were chasing him for doing graffiti and he jumped off the bridge into the Chicago River." I gave Mi'jo my condolences at the loss of another friend and he shrugged. David, the young man who was to go to college with him, didn't make it either. One morning in the early fall of their freshman year, I woke to find Mi'jo standing at the threshold of his room. He had started staying in the dorm so I was caught by surprise. He called out to me, "David's dead, Ma." I never got the details. Like generations of Chicago kids following my own generation, Mi'jo had come to take early death in stride.

BARGAINING

His attorney was optimistic. My son had not demonstrated greed (most of the money was recovered), possessed a weapon, nor made threats. Very importantly, in the eyes of the court he had the support of family and friends. Mi'jo had been depressed for a very long time and as I came to see it, had turned to drugs to self-medicate. In addition, if he started in high school while his brain was still forming, and if he had a predisposition to addiction, it was no wonder that by his midtwenties the abuse was well established.

Nevertheless, Mi'jo was taken away to do his time. He had accepted his guilt from the start. The attorney assured me my son was a college-educated young and intelligent guy with a lot of future ahead. Given the long-term penalties for felons, I thought, one could only hope.

DEPRESSION

A year and one month after my son's incarceration, I was firmly entrenched in Kübler-Ross's fourth stage of grief: depression. My inner conflict with organized religion remained, but the reality was that my spirituality gave me solace. One aspect of my spirituality comes from nature, my environment, and people whose priority it is to respect life on the planet.

The day after Christmas 2011, I took a drive up north in New Mexico, where I make one of my homes. A professor friend invited me to his pueblo, Ohkay Owingeh, to watch the turtle dance in which he was participating. The dance is part of a long ceremony, which may include vision quests to the mountains, days of ritual in the kivas, and fasting among the males of the tribe.

The people there are Pueblo (the Spanish word for "town"); they speak Tewa and, of course, English. It is thought the Pueblo people came up north from México and were of Aztec origin. The name of the reservation was originally San Juan, applied by the notoriously cruel colonizer Juan de Oñate. It is a testament to the human spirit that any Indians have survived to see today. The Pueblos have revived their ceremonies; memory is a path to self-preservation.

Living in New Mexico, I feel a profound connection to my ancestors and an awareness of location as a continuum. Spanish and Indians fought hard. Their progeny, Mexicans fought them and whites hard. Africans, like the famous slave Estevan who traveled with Oñate, mixed their blood, too. Today, as then (and long before when clan fought clan), our aim has been to survive—and thrive.

My friends and I arrived on a cloud-laden day before sunset to find fifty men and boys of all ages in formation, shoulder to shoulder, each wearing a turtle shell behind the right knee that made it sound like rain. Among the dancers were spring and summer people. Sometimes they are called the Turquoise and Squash people. Where once they wore the feathers of birds they'd caught and pigs' hooves attached to the tops of their leather thongs, the costumes in modern times are replaced with synthetic fabrics, jingle bells, and other store-bought adornments. As they danced solemnly they sang as generations had before them. Deep male voices resonated off nearby mountains.

Men perform the sacred turtle dance for the winter solstice. Their songs usher in the New Year, which is, in fact, not new but an endless cycle of nature, tradition, and beliefs. The turtle represents mother earth and precious water. Its hard shell represents perseverance and protection. It has been used as a calendar. The thirteen large patterned squares in the center of the shell represent the thirteen full moons of the year. The twenty-eight smaller squares around the perimeter of the shell represent the twenty-eight days of each lunar month. Thus, indigenous thought is tied to nature in a myriad of ways.

That afternoon, in the skin of the young men, strong warriors of their people, I saw my absent and much-longed-for son. In their muscular limbs built for running, carrying, hunting, and protecting, I yearned for his presence. I thirsted for his freedom but also for the saving of his spirit. In the shocks of black hair standing like flint arrows, I saw Mi'jo's. In their earnest calls and vigorous uniform movements I wished to find him. Yes, that one there! Mi'jo!

These boys, young and not so young men, were not without their problems, either. Their small adobe homes were patched and tilted. Skinny dogs wandered. Depression, drugs, teen delinquency, pregnancies, and suicide hit scandalous heights in these segregated communities in the United States, consequences of a dignified people devastated by invaders. I heard the timbre of the men's chants and my heart was filled with their courage and aspirations. They, with their sacrifices, vigor, and medicine songs, were reenforcing themselves—each other and those of us watching—against a still-hostile outside world.

I was coming down with a terrible cold. In my mucus-filled stupor I'd left home in the lumber jacket I used around my ranchito when collecting kindling to start the morning fire and to feed the mares. It was my son's when he was twelve, the age he passed me in height. As the last glimmer of day faded and the dancers stopped and went to pray in the kiva, spectators, mostly from the pueblo, dispersed. My friends and I wandered over to a man from Santo Domingo

Pueblo selling his jewelry and some blankets at a foldout table. The blankets were no longer loom woven as in times past but factory made. I bought two, one for me and one for my son.

Right then, I noticed a couple of tourists. There were very few around that day; these looked like college girls from India. For some reason, seeing Southeast Asian Indians on a Native American reservation in the United States was poignant to me. It was a visual association of how far-reaching colonialism had been. The girls were coming out of the sixteenth-century Catholic church. I ducked inside to pray. It was dimly lit and empty. In her elegant book *Full of Grace: Encountering Mary in Faith, Art, and Life*, Judith Dupré writes there is nothing quite like the feeling one has when finding oneself entirely alone in a church. The Catholic churches on the pueblos are not gilded but late sixteenth- and seventeenth-century tributes to colonizing the New World.

The icons were carved of wood, and the sad labor of the enslaved indigenous still reeked in the vigas and stucco walls. The lights released a soft glow, creating both a sense of eeriness and peace simultaneously. I made my way to the first pew to kneel and have a better view of the altar with its Crucifixion and saints. As a mixed-race woman, I've honored all the gods of my ancestors.

My heart was heavy.

For so many years I had fought with everything in me to

prove that a single mother could successfully raise a boy of color. I knew there were those who did. One produced the mayor of San Antonio! Where had I gone wrong? There in that dark historical building I questioned myself to the core. Had I held my head too high and gained God's disapproval because of the sin of pride? Had I not held it high enough and allowed society's prejudices to undermine my authority in my son's life? Had not employing corporal punishment (as my mother once advocated) backfired? Should I have *insisted* he go to live with his father when he was a head taller than me and nearly everyone opined that a boy that age should be under a man's supervision?

Mi'jo had finished an honor's high school program and university degree with as much ease as some kids did skateboard tricks. It wasn't until after the age of twenty-six that he was taken down by the ever-testing gods or society. Had it only been a matter of time, then? Should I see it from a Chicana feminist perspective? I wondered. The game of postcolonization was not, despite his education, a game my son recognized. If I could be accused of having protected him too much, what did it mean that his father had scarcely bothered to protect his son at all? In that dark, cold church, I even questioned all my questions.

My weeping echoed. My tearful eyes searched the flicker of dim candles, the silence of the place, and still no answers came. I prayed fervently for clarity and felt none come to me. I had devoted myself for over a quarter of a century to being a mother and I had failed at the most important duty.

After a time, I wiped my face and made my way slowly out. I was mourning a child once issued from my womb, now gone, lost to me. A beloved doesn't have to die for you to grieve their absence. They only have to stray too far from your reach.

ACCEPTANCE

When Mi'jo was first arrested I received collect calls. The first words he spoke were, "I'm sorry, Mom." I didn't know what to say, but given the circumstances there wasn't much opportunity, in any case. It was extremely difficult to write to him at first. In fact, it was hard to write at all, even in my journal. My heart, or where my heart had once been, ached too much to so much as pick up a pen. When I did finally get a letter off, my son said he had trouble reading my hand-writing. Eventually he went to a facility where emails were allowed. We began to email every day. I sent books—many—including my own titles and he soon began to read (again). Over time, he was reading, writing, retaining information—connecting.

Two months before his release, but facing another Christmas locked up, he said, "I was thinking about Pachelbel's Canon in D Major. I really liked playing it on the cello. You should check it out, Mamá."

There was a pause on my end.

"Ma?"

"Mi'jo," I struggled against limited minutes to say what raced through my head at the moment. "I haven't heard you speak of the music you used to play in . . . what? Seven years?" It was more like ten.

"Yeah, yeah," he said.

Slowly over the two years of his incarceration I saw him return in speech, attention span, and even long-dismissed goals. He was reading all the time. I'd send books, those he asked for and others I'd recommend. Sometimes, I'd read my own copy at home so we could talk about them. He started teaching a creative writing class under my long-distance direction. He found he liked playwriting. His writing skills improved and he began contributing thoughtful reviews for my online zine.

One difficult book that I ordered for each of us was a slender collection of poems called *A Toast in the House of Friends* by Akilah Oliver. It was difficult because of her story; her poems were exquisite. The collection was written in memoriam to her only child, a son who died at twenty-one. Oluchi (who would have been a year older than my son) was a graffiti artist in Los Angeles when he went to the ER suffering from stomach pain. He died on a gurney in the waiting area.

A few years later Akilah Oliver passed, too, of apparent heart failure—but I knew it was a broken heart. At first, I'd open the paperback, see the graphics of her dead child's graffiti, and I could not bear to read this mother's anguish over his lifestyle. She, too, had been opposed to her son's tagging. She forced herself after his death to view the walls he painted and included the color plates in the book. The volume stayed next to my bed for months unread. Meanwhile, my son devoured his copy.

He embraced the experimental prose-poetry style of his "Aki," as he referred to her later, and wrote a very good essay about it. Mi'jo had become enthusiastic about literature, writing, and even acting. I encouraged it all via emails and calls as I always encouraged anything that had to do with intellectual stimulation. Mi'jo asked for art books, those on Jean-Michel Basquiat in particular, the young French Haitian artist whose Warhol-associated rise ended abruptly with drug abuse. Both Oliver and Basquiat would have rejected being associated with graffiti culture and yet, my son felt their influence on hip-hop culture. He wrote a piece about Basquiat too, which we also published in *La Tolteca*, a zine I started in 2010 just before his incarceration. Through books and writing, I had found a way in to him again. And more ideas were coming to him every day. He returned to an earlier goal, law school. An attorney friend sent him a guide to study for the LSAT and recommended he spend time in the legal library.

There is yet much more to look at when telling the story of one son's spiral and one mother's heartache: the Big Picture. Globalization has affected most of the world. It allows for illicit gross profits from the drug industry while the majority of the planet's population lives in poverty. In a country proud of its wealth and resources, healthcare and public education are not guaranteed to all citizens.

Without making excuses for any individual's bad behavior, here is some societal context. The robbery that landed Mi'jo in prison was committed at the height of the recession. We lost most of our savings that were in stocks, bonds, and investments. Like so many among the middle class, we trusted banks and our government with safekeeping our futures. During that same time, I was diagnosed with cancer, unemployed, and without medical insurance. Real estate values dropped and rents went up. New post-9/11 industries cropped up to exploit the new "War on Terrorism." Citizens experienced increased surveillance, diminished civil liberties, and outright harassment by authorities. College graduates found themselves with no jobs and school loans to pay. The chasm between the wealthy and the rest of us widened. The proverbial American Dream for the average person evaporated. Yet, we were made to feel that, somehow, if we just went along with the program, each of us would soon be all right again. Our families would be fine. Instead the reality was that many of us gave up loved ones to the military, drug wars, and the incarceration industries. These blows wouldn't be easy to recover from.

Yet, we push on.

I remember telling a close friend, who was more like

family and knew my son, about Mi'jo's arrest. At first he grew pale at the distressful news. Then he shared some comforting words that proved prophetic. "You may not see it this way now, but this is *not* the worst that could have happened," he said. "In reality, it was God's way of saving your son's life."

With all endings come beginnings. We began counting the days until Mi'jo's release.

Mi'jo and I reunited (Chicago; 2013).

Love, Your Son, Marcello

My son and I emailed regularly throughout his incarceration. Over the many months, we were able to connect about ideas, words, and family. As hard as it was, there was also joy as I begin to glimpse Mi'jo again.

FROM: Marcello Castillo
DATE: October 30, 2011

No one has been writing to me or emailing since my sentencing and I have been getting a little lonely.

I am reading another book by Tom Robbins, who I like, and I found a really cool section in *USA Today* concerned with nonprofits that help women across the world—you know, goat farms and HIV awareness, child brides and prostitution. I am also reading about solar energy. The world is in a very greedy state but, like you have always said, it is good to pick a cause and stick to it. I like the word you use, conscientación.

I am learning the hard way that sex isn't everything, having a child is a life-changing event, and it is okay to be alone. Stay strong for me!

FROM: Ana Castillo
DATE: November 1, 2011

Mi'jo querido: How are you? Today we begin to think of our past loved ones. I think it is also a good time for us to think and meditate on those who cannot be with us today. Your small child for the time being has lost her daddy—and you, her. It isn't the worst tragedy (it's not forever), but it is enough time that we suffer your loss.

It was your first serious relationship, intense, passionate, and ultimately catastrophic—as often such first loves end. But there is much life ahead to employ the lessons learned and future relationships will benefit from your experience, hopefully.

I pray for you each day, Mi'jito lindo. Stay strong and know your life awaits.

FROM: Marcello Castillo
DATE: November 18, 2011

I just got out from a Christian life skills class.

I'm trying to do programs that will give me some type of transferable work experience. Dad sent me some info about the lawyer thing and the short answer is that I can't be a lawyer with a felony. I can't vote either, apparently. I would need to be pardoned, get my record expunged, or get permission from the bar association to practice.

I'm afraid I ruined my chances by this careless crime.

FROM: Ana Castillo
DATE: November 29, 2011

If we learn from our mistakes then that is a good thing.

I read online that your conviction would probably not be the type to be expunged. First-time drug offenses are but, even then, all that takes lawyers and time. Still, I would not close the thought of a law career just yet.

FROM: Marcello Castillo
DATE: December 1, 2011

I just read the play *Short Eyes* by Miguel Piñero. It was a classic! I was inspired by their story as an acting group but also because my favorite hip-hop group, The Wu-Tang Clan, sampled the movie *Short Eyes* in their album *The W* (one of my favorites)! It is cool to make all these connections between the things I hold sacred! I read in one of the Basquiat books that Warhol wrote a book about becoming a famous painter called *POPism*. They all seemed like a bunch of party animals that made being cool really marketable. Doing drugs, painting whatever came to their minds. The reason he called his studio "The Factory" was because they cranked out artwork. Tonight I am going to sign up for an art class. There might be a way to get supplies just yet!

FROM: Ana Castillo
DATE: December 1, 2011

Mi'jo: It's good to see you're not just positive and optimistic but "alert." In the past your emails always sounded that way so I must say, it was part of my great shock a year ago to find out the contrary.

I hope you are not just putting on a happy face for me.

Back in the day I was acquainted with Piñero. He was very strung out. Because of his talent and being in New York, however, he made some major professional connections. He worked with Joseph Papp and also wrote for the TV show *Miami Vice*. My friend Prof. N. said, "It takes a village," regarding the support team I'm putting together for you. But you must remember when you are out to be a good friend to the people who've helped you, however you can.

FROM: Marcello Castillo
SENT: December 23, 2011

I'm good. Just taking it one day at a time. We are slowly being let out of lockdown. We get one hot meal and we get to be in the dayroom until 3:30–4 p.m.

On a lighter note, I showed some Chicano "friends" here your books. One of them, whose dad was a bodyguard for Corky Gonzalez, wants to send you some money to send some of your books, signed, to his mom in Denver, CO. He has seen your poetry books and is checking out *Sapogonia*. My barber here is reading *Loverboys* and one of the books of poetry. They also loved the Zeta Acosta books and the guy from Denver kept saying, "Que viva la raza, que viva Zeta!"

FROM: Marcello Castillo
DATE: January 11, 2012

I just got the okay to teach a creative writing class. I also signed up for a beginning guitar class. I went today but realized it is the same time as my writing class will be. Still, it was really fun and all the hand confidence came back to me. It really lifted my spirits to play again.

I pray to myself to have the strength to see this through, pray to the universe, and pray to God to make me strong and wise enough to focus on the prize of my daughter outside these gates. Like you said, I am just getting by here.

Well, Madre mía, I am going to lie down and get ready for a new day. I am in a new place in my head and my life; I want to be taken seriously.

FROM: Ana Castillo
SENT: January 12, 2012

Mi querido hijo: How are you today? Do you ever get to go outside? I wonder, although I don't expect for you to tell me, if there is a lot of tension?

Let me know if you want feedback on how to run your class. Read about the basic structure of stories—the beginning, middle, and the end; the crisis and resolution; etc. And read stories looking for that arc. Most writing books have exercises. Pick some out, assign them in the workshop, and give a certain amount of time to write in class, ten or twenty minutes. Sometimes they can read out loud and share what they came up with.

I have good news for you, Hijo—you have a new friend. She is the Chicana attorney I told you about. She said she is very happy to support Chicanos who want to go into law because she said we need them badly.

FROM: Marcello Castillo
DATE: January 24, 2012

Wowee! I had a crazy dream last night. We were at our old place and our dog wanted to go out. I put the dog on the leash. There was a hyena out in the back parking lot, but it was tame. I think the most significant thing about the dream was how I looked forward to taking out the dog and didn't think of it as a chore. We went walking around the whole neighborhood. Then, I found the jacket that my godmother Linda from Berkeley bought for me, and it was covered in spray paint. I showed it to you and we both wondered where the stains came from because all the clothes in my closet were nice dress clothes, like khaki slacks and jackets. Maybe I was working out some issues I have always had with being lazy and doing graff art.

What could I have been had I pursued more productive hobbies?

FROM: Ana Castillo
DATE: February 4, 2012

Well, we are here at the threshold of life's possibilities.

The mares are free today and thrilled, running around. It is sunny, about sixty degrees. I'm tied to my desk, determined to get through this writing.

Everyone is feeling the recession. I sent out an e-blast to about two thousand people and not one person responded to my workshops.

When you get out you will be in a halfway house and find many challenges. I hope you don't get depressed, discouraged, and end in a slump. You must see it as a step *up* toward being free.

Read Dostoyevsky's *Crime and Punishment.* He is one of my favorites. The novel is about sin and redemption. Once you are free, you are free, Son.

FROM: Marcello Castillo
DATE: February 5, 2012

How R U this morning?

Just feeling really at peace and not letting anything bother me because I have one year left! ;-)> Your latest email really cheered me up because it really feels like a future filled with possibilities. I was up late last night just reading and thinking about what I want to do when I get out. It is definitely a privilege to be able to live one's life responsibly and not as a chore, as I previously thought. I've realized the key to living a fulfilling life is finding those things that you really love in your situation. In my case here it is chess, writing, reading, yoga, eating healthy, and exercising. If I can find true joy in what I find myself doing for work–i.e., ESL or GED teacher, eventually a counselor–I can find the acts of doing those jobs as rewards in themselves. I think it is a very mature perspective. Thanks!

FROM: Marcello Castillo
DATE: February 24, 2012

Can you see how much *Oscar "Zeta" Acosta: The Uncollected Works* are on Amazon.com? He and Bukowski are two of my favorite writers. I heard Zeta was considered a failure as a poet?

FROM: Ana Castillo
DATE: March 5, 2012

I'm not sending you a million books.[1] To be a writer–bad, mediocre, good, or once-in-a-century brilliant–you must *love* literature and to read. I only mention sending books because of that reason.

I got a disturbing email from X. X is talented and bright but tends to have serious addictions. Addictive behavior, Son, whether alcohol, drugs, pills, or weed, is destructive to a person's life and to your loved ones. If you transfer such addictions to chasing

---

1. I did, in fact, send Bukowski's poetry to him. At that time, I bought Bukowsi's fiction to read. His work ended up inspiring me to start writing a new work. It became the novel *Give It to Me*. Sometimes, Mi'jo and I read the same books in order to discuss. One of these was the memoir *One Day It'll All Make Sense* by one of Mi'jo's favorite rappers, Common.

women online or playing poker, it's the same thing. That is why I say you must stay with therapy when you get out.

FROM: Marcello Castillo
DATE: March 13, 2012

I have a question for you. What alternatives do we have to patriarchy? A matriarchy? Anarchy? I have always been intrigued with the idea of a new religion or a new societal structure. I hoped you would explore it further in your novel *Sapogonia*. But like you've said, "An arrival is always a point of departure," which is where the novel led you.

FROM: Ana Castillo
DATE: March 14, 2012

We cannot think of any monumental change in the world without thinking about patriarchy, which is capitalism's fundamental basis. I am a poet, not a politician. In my poet's mind and vision, which at the onset I'll admit is mostly wishful thinking, if we began considering what was good for most of the world's organic population and what was beneficial to the planet's restoration and well-being, we would be on the way to an alternative to patriarchy. What that alternative will look like in the future will depend on so much that we can only let our minds imagine.

When we think of the good of most living creatures on the planet and the planet itself, alternatives and solutions will come from many sources. Male (hetero, macho) dominance and presumed superiority would not be the rule or expectation for those solutions. When it is not considered the first and most "credible" source then, we have moved away from patriarchy.

What that will mean to a new world economic basis and what it would be called, I don't know. But it would mean that women would not be products or conspirators but active agents of change. You may say, well, plenty of women participate in the economy now. When women use their femaleness in society, such as entertainers like J. Lo or Beyoncé, and then claim they have become "power players," they are doing no more than supporting and promoting patriarchal and capitalist goals. It's complicated. And as long as a few people, like those examples, are enjoying astronomical benefits and cast their blinding starlight on the throngs of wishful spectators (while wars, sweatshops, and world hunger continue), nothing much is going to change.

FROM: Marcello Castillo
DATE: May 16, 2012

Pit Bull Puppy Love

I was heartbroken
Like a 15-year-old Rottweiler Love

The day I Real Eyes'd that GRAFF was my disease
I didn't want a career.
I didn't care about getting paid.
I just wanted to smoke bluntz and
F*CK $#!T UP! Total Destruction! PURE DELINQUENCE!
The Uglier The Fillz
The Better.
As long as the person who owned it
(the property, that is)
had to grind their fingertips to the bone gristle
to clean off my name!
Just paint over it!
Just Call the City, they'll buff it!
Just replace the whole window!
It didn't matter because it wasn't mine!
I didn't work for it.
Why should I CARE?
Then I grew up and figured out
that I was destroying myself faster
than the walls I hated so much!

FROM: Marcello Castillo
DATE: July 30, 2012

Como estás, mi mamá?

I am doing okay. I worked today. I got a receipt of acceptance for the writings I entered in the PEN prisoner writing competition.[2]

FROM: Ana Castillo
DATE: November 10, 2012

Your incarceration may have inadvertently given you a second lease on life. With the lease, show a new appreciation of God's blessings.

Your poems give me the inspiration to keep doing the work I have ahead.

xo love,
Tu madre que te ama incondicionalmente

FROM: Marcello Castillo
DATE: November 11, 2012
SUBJECT: Revised Basquiat essay[3]

Jean-Michel Basquiat's career began with the inception of his graffiti street-poet alter ego "SAMO" c. 1977 and continued until his untimely death from a drug overdose in 1988.

Basquiat had an acute political mind. He openly mocked the

2. Mi'jo won third place.
3. The following is an excerpt of a draft of the essay Mi'jo wrote and ran for *La Tolteca*.

established art world with what he perceived as its frivolity and exuberant pricing. *Five Thousand Dollars* (1982) is a black rectangular splash over a drab brown background with the words and numbers "five thousand dollars" ($5000) in black and white. It is the asking price.

He staunchly denied being a graffiti writer. However, in my opinion, Basquiat was one, or at least to some degree, his work shows its influence. Basquiat saw the raw power that graffiti had as public art and began tagging the moniker "SAMO," short for "Same Ol' Shit." It was also a variation for the racist term "Sambo" and an anagram of Amos (from the TV show *Amos 'n' Andy*, seen by some critics of how blacks were portrayed in white society as a variation of Step 'n Fetchit characters.) What set Basquiat apart from many graffiti writers was that he deliberately used graffiti as a platform to position himself within the New York art scene. Basquiat did not garner much support from African Americans while alive. Most of his collectors were affluent whites.

FROM: Ana Castillo
DATE: November 22, 2012

Buenos días, hijo mio:
I am grateful today, Thanksgiving, that we have made it through the greatest trial of our lives, Son.
Say your prayers today and do your yoga. Consider today as the beginning of your countdown.

xo love,
    Tu madre que te extraña mucho

FROM: Marcello Castillo
DATE: November 22, 2012

Happy Thanksgiving! :D>
Thank you for your positivity! I truly appreciate it. Send me
The New Jim Crow book you mentioned. I am thankful for a strong
and intelligent Mamá!

Love, your son,
    Marcello

*Mi'jo was released February 14, 2013. He began a job busing
tables while in the halfway house as he pursued the goals mentioned here. He was released early from probation. At this writing, he remains sober and is employed full-time at a grassroots
organization where he works with people requiring assistance
transitioning to the workplace. He is a devoted part-time single
father. Equipped now with a paralegal certificate he earned since
his release, he is making plans to pursue a career in law. In his
spare time, among quiet activities, he enjoys reading.*

Me at home in New Mexico (2015).

And the Woman Fled into the Desert

And the woman fled into the desert,
there to be cared for, for 1,260 days,
in a place which God had prepared for her.

—Revelation 12:6

It is over a decade since I left Chicago to live in the Chihuahuan desert. Some years I've been in my homestead part-time, but with the recession (and loss of full-time employment) it became my permanent residence. There have been many extended hours of writing in that place.

Once I was asked by a literary periodical what I could see from my window. From the mistress bedroom, windows facing east, I have a view of the Franklin Mountains. The Franklins comprise a small range that extends from the state line of New Mexico through El Paso, Texas. They may well be over a billion years old. At first glance of this expanse of mostly sedimentary rock, they appear rather unimpressive.

Sitting on my bed, laptop propped, I have watched those low mountains throughout entire days from sunrise to sunset, during heavy rains, obscured by dust storms, and throughout many clear days. Over time, I've learned that the Franklins are not unimpressive at all. The humongous earth spirit they represent has spoken to me with each shape-shift and color they undertake. They have kept vigil through two novels and countless hours working on much more. Sometimes, I add music to the mix, old-school CDs piped through speakers—arias, boleros, new age, salsa, and standard jazz classics have served as a sound track for these periods of solitude and focus on my work.

Life outside harmonizes with the CDs. Before the few pine trees around the house were nearly all annihilated by blight, there was a symphony of birds' songs from dawn until dusk. When I had more trees, I watched the myriad of birds headed to nest and settle in for the night. The same chickadee woke me each day before sunrise. And throughout the day chirps did indeed fill my heart with song.

The light of the desert accompanies me, too. There's nothing like it. (The sun by the sea may be *as* thrilling but not more.) In summer, so bright and combined with the heat, however, the sun makes you feel as if you've had your eyelids peeled back. I swear there is such a thing as eyeball burn. But mostly the light seems to play tricks on you. See the way it hits the wall there? See how it has changed the room since the morning? Outdoors, all of desert nature is in high relief. Periodically, you can hear the whistle of the Rio Grande and El Paso Railroad Company trains rumbling through at a distance.

My home sits on a mesa facing the Franklins. As the mesa declines, there are the verdant crops of small farms in summer and, farthest below, the town of Anthony. It serves as the dividing line between New Mexico and Texas. To the south is El Paso and to the north are the colonias—villages that lead to Las Cruces. What I see from my windows as the day has folded into night and I have been at the computer working since sunrise is a stream of twinkling lights below. The stark light fades to black slowly, leaving in its wake dogs barking and the occasional howling of coyotes.

The dogs lie about all day and after dark join the canine choir throughout the mesa. In winter (a winter that seems to grow longer and colder each year), they come inside and throw themselves down in front of the wood-burning stove in the living room. If permitted by the smallest one that sleeps with me, they sneak into my bedroom and loll around the bed. We all listen to the barking of less fortunate dogs left outside and howling coyotes until we go to sleep in the lonesome quiet of the desert.

There are military surveillance planes from the White Sands Missile Range or Fort Bliss that fly overhead occasionally intruding on the isolation. When the mares of my modest (near-barren) ranchito are let out of their corral, there is nothing more exciting than the sounds of their hooves against the sandy floor running free. Sometimes winds carry the yells of the neighbors playing basketball; I hear the thump-thump of dribbling and the banter of boys becoming men.

There used to be a small grove of pecan trees next door to me. The tree keepers who resided in a trailer on that land would every now and then raise a ruckus with a family party. Mexican banda or norteño music played. Kids shouted from an inflatable bounce house, drunk male voices carried over, everything blaring against the stark light of the desert until dark. Disrupting my peace and the illusion that there I was free from gauche society, it all used to annoy me. Then the lovely grove went dry—the draught. The family moved out and their decrepit trailer was razed. Now, when I think of it all, I miss the vitality of those families; they lived unfettered by pretenses. I don't miss their dogs.

One time I was walking my small Chihuahua-terrier mix when their two Rottweiler's crossed under the barbed-wire fence. I scooped up my yapping puppy, who'd now gone into fierce guard mode, and held him tight as they, growling, kept keen eyes fixed on him. I didn't know what I was going to do next, but when I yelled for them to "GIT!" their owner came out and peace was once again restored on the mesa. Generally, except for the occasional rattlesnake sighting, my walks around the patch of desert I have called home are uneventful.

One warm night I was driving up the mesa to my casita. Suddenly my eye caught the shimmering of small lights out on a field, like a slow flurry of large fireflies. Along the dirt road, old cars were parked. Here and there a woman stood outside rocking a child. It was onion-picking season. Because of the excruciating heat, people were hired to work at night. The fireflies were miners' lights strapped around their foreheads. At night, better temperatures eased the backbreaking repetitive effort of pulling onions out of the earth, though you might also run across a rattler, scorpion, spider, or other nighttime prowler.

Once, a neighbor set up a camera to catch a glimpse of what was devouring small animals and leaving their carcasses on their field. It was a mountain lion. After that, in my bed at night, I devised a plan: if I caught sight of that mountain lion peering into my room, which has many long windows, I'd run to the bathroom or to the garage and barricade myself inside. Outside, of course, there'd be no escape.

Although before this recent life I was mostly a city dweller, I do have early memories that were triggered by those field workers. My mother's younger sister was widowed very young. Tía Flora was born in Mexico City but moved near the border of Laredo and lived in Nuevo Laredo in her late teens, joining my mother and their grandparents who had migrated earlier. The sisters were orphans. My aunt's second husband, a card-carrying Tejano, came from a farm-worker family. They migrated throughout the year following the crops. Every summer they made it to Indiana, which is close to Chicago where I am from, and they stayed in the labor camp.

From the visits we paid to see my tía Flora's in-laws in summer during tomato season in Indiana, I vividly recall the conditions that Mexicans and American Mexicans experienced in labor camps. While picking the fruits and vegetables that would stock grocery shelves and would be sent to canneries (where more Mexicans worked) and eventually reached American tables, the workers existed in squalor.

I don't like to think of those labor-camp visits. Although I was just a kid, una escuincle of six or eight years of age, not knowing anything from anything else, growing up in a deteriorated neighborhood in Chicago that was about to get torn down, I knew the place *that* family was staying in was perpetually dark. It was a scary, dismal place for a child.

A bulb hung from the ceiling in the middle of the room. I don't recollect any windows. There was no refrigeration and no outlets for fans. Maybe six adults slept in that room. In Chicago in our flat, we had big rats that chased the house cat. Sometimes kerosene ran out on winter nights and we slept with layers of clothes on, but the labor camp brought Mexican daily life to a different dimension. Sometimes you hear people speak of their impoverished childhood and they say, "We didn't know we were poor." I think they only mean they felt secure in the love they had from family because, when you go to bed hungry, you never forget it.

As children playing on Sundays in the labor camp,

somehow we wandered to the ranch owners' home. We snuck around the pool area and played house in the cabana. Sparkling pools, sprawling private dwellings with trimmed hedges, and something so utterly luxurious like a place to change into your swimsuit belonged exclusively to white people. They were monolingual and ate Wonder Bread slices off little plates at dinner tables. Their fingernails were clean and their children got on yellow school buses and went to schools with teachers who looked like them. They would become policemen, firemen, and nurses, like those in our schoolbooks. None of those doors were open to us, because we were brown.

Many years later when I was in Germany defending my dissertation, I ended up in a serious discussion in the streamlined, Scandinavian-style kitchen of a woman scholar who had been a great supporter of my work. She was a Marxist. We were discussing racism. She tried to comprehend by sharing how difficult it was living in a village where there were serious divisions between Christians and her family. Her family subscribed to no religion, which made them everyone's targets. They were marginalized as a minority. I thought I was gaining ground on the added layers of prejudice regarding issues around ethnicity and race when she stopped me flatly with the left argument: "Don't you think it's really all about class?"

I was left bug-eyed. Colonialism and its legacies were largely based on exploiting other human beings through racism. Racism and ethnicity weren't incidental to class. How could she not see that?

At the labor camp, as opposed to the ranch house, there was no doubt it was a Mexican world. Perhaps there was a hot plate for the doña's tortilla making, my tía's traveling mother-in-law. As for running water, I remember a large communal something that in my mind's faded memory looks like a trough. In my head I hear people laughing at that trough as they come with their bushels of picked tomatoes. The workers were paid by the bushel. Children were paid less than adults for the same bushel. I see the sun-grazed faces of brown children, the faces of my older half siblings among them. My mother sent them, around eleven or thirteen years old, to work for a few weeks in summer. Instead of going away to summer camp for free with Jane Addams's Hull House, they were picking fruit for a few cents a bushel. Did they also stay in that shack with my aunt's in-laws, a roomful of adults and nearly adults, who only worked and slept until a day of exhausted rest on Sunday? I'm sure of it.

It was on these Sundays when I visited with my tía, cousins, and my mamá. We were there to pick up my older siblings or to drop them off. In Chicago my mother, too, worked all week, in a factory. Someone (my aunt's husband? Did he have a car?) must have given us a ride out to the country so that we could see our family in labor camps. We drove past Indiana oil refineries blowing out toxic gases that thickened the air. Those refineries left a stench in their wake but lured anyone needing work. Without a doubt, the drones were mostly Latinos. They might not make foreman or floor manager and they might not always be welcome in a union, but they were there working toward the American Dream, nonetheless. In the fields, farm laborers didn't have to work on Sundays, if they didn't "want" to. But my memory of people lugging bushels around that trough-like water source tells me many did.

When I was thirteen, my father brought home a large King James Bible from his factory job at a bindery company. They were not giving them away and, no doubt, he got it out past the guard under his coat. His friends were always taking things that they made at factories to sell to each other. Very likely they considered it their due for the paltry wages. One guy sold us the blankets that were used to wrap furniture in moving vans. You could hardly stir in bed under the weight and stiffness of those things, but they did keep us warm.

No one in my family had interest in the Bible, or any other book my dad snuck home—textbooks or random nonfiction like the *Betty Crocker Cookbook* or *The Life of Elijah*. My parents set up a metal bookshelf, perhaps in hopes that those daunting units of information would serve one of us kids in our schoolwork. I also think my parents liked the display as home decor.

I'm sure it wouldn't come as a surprise to anyone now that I read most, if not all, the books. I was the only one in the household who did. I still have the well-worn cookbook, too. The Bible, however, was a veritable treasure of story-telling, igniting a lifetime fascination with fantastic narratives. My father told stories all the time, but those ancients of the Hebrew world were masters of magical realism. I say this although I did believe in God, and sometimes still do, and if God's voice actually emitted from a burning bush or if Adam truly lived past eight hundred years, it's not for me to argue. It was, after all, once upon a time and so long ago.

The edition also contained a great many pictures of classic oil paintings. When I remember that trough and the field workers of the labor camp, the children's laughter and women with their dark tresses rinsing out bushels of dirty tomatoes, I think of the Gospel of John, when Jesus came upon a woman of Samaria and asked her for a drink. After a brief discourse, he convinced her that he had brought the Word of God and whoever heard it would never again be thirsty. The paintings were luscious and I would see some of them again much later as an art major, in slides in art history in state college. Some I would see in paintings around the world. In my memories, those dark women in ragged dresses (it was before jeans and shorts became acceptable for women) all seem to be the Samarian woman, blissful in the ignorance of a certain truth. Perhaps, in this case, the truth was of capitalism's disastrous promise.

They say a novel begins with a query. On a frosty morning one January, as I sipped my coffee from the window by the kitchen sink, I watched the snow layering the Franklins, white over dark magenta. NPR's morning radio was playing in the background. My life in that place had become mostly one of stark aloneness. There were the animals and the strange way the desert made you feel like nothing was happening, all the while teeming with life, but it would be another day void of human company.

I could hear the menacing howls of the wind that started the night before. The temperatures in the mountains had to have been threatening to whoever might find themselves out there. They would have crossed from México and, if they made it alive, into El Paso. What if they hadn't? What if they got lost? Or what if any of the two- or four-footed predators searching out such vulnerable targets caught up with them? Such devastating images aren't hard to come by. Countless bad and good films have been made of these treacherous journeys of not only Mexicans but also others who seek work in a different country but aren't able to obtain visas. They don't cross borders illegally on a whim. Even when many apply for permits, they don't receive them. The desire to be reunited with loved ones and the equally wrenching need to leave them behind impels the destitute to make that dangerous trek, too.

Later that day, for the sake of inspiration I switched off the talk radio and put on some music, Maria Callas or Tania Libertad singing "Deja que salga la luna." I watched the light change on the Franklins and thought of the countless people in the world who were born to live and die in anonymity, playing out lives no better or worse than anyone else's and no one noticing.

Sometimes we give others who don't make a big mark in some way a moment in the limelight in fiction. Our novelists' eyes and ears say to our readers, "Look here, please. Listen. This existence mattered, too." That morning, thinking of border crossings, I wondered what it would be like to be one of those individuals trying to make my way across and, for whatever reason, not making it. As I went to my laptop on the kitchen counter, a second query came to me. What would it be like to be on this side waiting for that missing loved one? Who would I call? Better yet, could I call anyone for assistance in finding him or her?

That day, I wrote what would become the first chapter of my next novel. I called it *The Guardians*. Like the Franklins, guardians keeping constant vigil, nearly everyone in the story fails to guide someone to safety at some point. When the novel came out, I went to read it at universities and book festivals, as I always do. It surprised me (and not in a good way) that for the first time in thirty years, since I read poetry as a labeled "radical woman of color," there were people in the audiences who would get up and walk out. The stories of Mexicans crossing illegally, told from the enraged perspective of those waiting on this side, was (to some) not worthy of compassion.

Similarly, *Massacre of the Dreamers*, my book of critical

essays on Xicanisma, which was published by a university press and for which I received a doctorate and, later, an honorary doctorate, provoked hostility. Getting it published had been difficult. I think it was because I wrote from the gut. For a long time, women of color in this country from modest backgrounds weren't supposed to be seen or heard. They were only meant to keep the assembly lines running without complaint, like my beautiful indigenous mamá did.

Some ten years after *Massacre of the Dreamers* came out, I went to work on an updated edition. The data I had put together with tedious effort and no funding, long before the Internet, seemed to be rapidly changing. By the year 2000, six years after the first edition was released with the new census results, all I heard was how Latinos were taking over the nation. With numbers, perhaps, but otherwise I didn't see it around me.

Meanwhile, women: Since the sixties, white feminists often compared their status to that of black men; this competition was given new life in the 2008 presidential election. It didn't surprise me that a man won the election. Nor that the political and academic discussion on race remained black and white, with white women representing what gains feminism had brought for women. Sitting in my desert retreat away from the hustle and bustle of urban life in those early years of the Obama administration, I wondered how much had actually changed concerning race and gender in the United States. With the new century came a desire to review my reflections on the current lives of women on both sides of the US-México border. Happily, the same university press that first published the book was interested in doing the new edition. They had no electronic copy of the first manuscript. (I may have had drafts stored in the form of floppy disks.) I undertook the laborious process of scanning each page and converting it with the use of an online platform to Word. It was not a neat conversion, with many misread symbols and poorly formatted pages. I went over each page, line by line, to clean it up. Tedious as this was, I found the process useful as I was also rewriting and updating the text.

The summer of 2012 I was at my desktop computer most days, scanning page after page. There were no windows in the study except for a sliding glass door, which was kept shut. There was no telling what might slither, squeeze, or fly through a crack. I'm not terribly afraid of all that creeps and crawls, but I prefer a certain distance. Once, while working in bed, a tiny ant that had settled on my soda can bit my upper lip when I tried to take a sip. The lip swelled immediately to distorted proportions. A call to the doctor, who said it was an allergic reaction, and a couple of further bites from such kind would surely be the cause of my death. Another time, having developed a healthy dread of near invisible ants, I woke in the middle of the night believing I had pulled out one crawling into my ear. Instead, I woke to find a small scorpion frantically running around the pillow without the tail I had apparently snapped off between my fingers. Suffice it to say, henceforth, I did not open the sliding door in the bedroom or the one in the study. Still, the house was kept at bearable temperatures with a swamp cooler and ceiling fan. Nothing stands out in memory during the months I worked this way on the project, apart from heat and solitude, except to say how utterly grateful I was to the gods the day I was done. Or nearly done, since no writer alive will concede to ever truly having finished a book.

Twenty years earlier, right after I was wrapping up the first edition, I wrote a novel. Because *Massacre* was a somber project, and in conjunction with prolonged periods of the solitude I've already mentioned, life seemed to call for some levity. While the book of essays had taken about seven years, the novel, *So Far from God*, was done quickly—in six months. Everything I had put down and qualified in essays was reimagined as fiction. I became the Samarian woman at the well telling my comadres and compadres of the strange and wondrous strangers who'd wandered by asking for a cool drink in exchange for their truth.

I started getting a little punchy again after finishing the new edition. I set upon a novel (eventually it became *Give It to Me*) to restore humor to my soul. With the startling red-orange sun making its ritual descent behind the flat horizon each night, while below in town twinkling lights went on in the Escándalo Night Club, I stayed at my computer and tried to find the funny in living. While I worked hard at writing humor, my life was not funny, not even in the ironic way one might say, "Funny, you should say that . . ."

To begin with, Mi'jo, several years out of college, was in jail. Since I had a cousin who served a sentence of twenty-one years, the two-year penalty my son received seemed merciful to a mother's heart. That summer, midway through his incarceration, it felt like twenty-one years.

In the evenings, after a day's work, I took advantage of the government-granted privilege of communication and sent my only child long electronic missives. I could write to him as much and as often as I wanted and not have to wait long for a response. Moreover, I could tell him everything that was on my mind. The emails were being read, of course, but what did a brokenhearted mother have to hide? With utter self-indulgence, I didn't hold back the hurt, confusion, and anger I'd had over his decisions. All the ranting may have done little to brighten my son's days, but it became a kind of release for me before bed.

During that first year, I tried to find a therapist I could talk to about my anguish and did do so a few times, but the cost of therapy without insurance was not easily shouldered. The adage "this too shall pass," which I was reminded of not from the Bible or a counselor but by my attorney, gave me the most comfort.

At times, my son's and my exchanges were not fraught with futile regrets or reproaches but discussions about writing, books, and music. From prison he began to write for my new arts and literary zine, *La Tolteca*. He won a writing award from PEN designated for the incarcerated. It wouldn't go on his resume later on—he had enough going against him with a record—but a writer getting an award from PEN is worth noting. He was in his own hell that summer. The inescapable heat, loneliness, and the anguish of my son's nonsensical loss of freedom meant I was in a purgatory of my own.

Anticlea, the mother of Odysseus, gave up on her son's return from the Trojan War; she died of grief. My son was no hero, to be sure. He was born to no throne. Nevertheless, I would hang in there and wait out his absence. All we have is the present, which comes to us moment by moment. That was then. This is now.

That summer, I stayed at my desk until late when sleep finally came to me. Mi'jo's imprisonment tormented me, and I thought a lot about the bizarre ten-year journey of Odysseus while his mother dwelled as a shadow in Hades. My understanding of the story of Odysseus is limited. (Unlike my son who read Homer in high school, I graduated from a secretarial school for girls that stressed typing speed above all else.) I have no formal studies in the classics. Nevertheless, from a rudimentary understanding, the story of Odysseus, like most mythology, intrigued me.

In myths, I have searched for the cultural seeds that make up men, women, and other wondrous creatures. In reading the story of Odysseus, I tried to understand how in every journey a man or woman was both hero and antihero at varying times. Years before, I taught a feminist class at a university using Joseph Campbell's model of the hero's journey to becoming savior or king. It was dismaying or perhaps, in the end, challenging, that I had to adjust women's history on such a journey.

Women did not share the linear narrative to leader (or failed potential leader). Instead, female archetypes had three life stages: lovely maiden, fertile mother, and (sterile, hunchbacked, saggy, wild-haired, banished from-the-village-to-a-hut-where-she-concocted-poisons-to-harm-men-unworthy-of-love-although-wise-and-yet-despised-for-her-wisdom) crone. Me, in other words.

Looking around, there I was, living in isolation at the edge of the world, which is what desert, sea, and sky have been to us for ages. I didn't concoct spells like the village witch, but I did enjoy cool herbal tea. As for the bad body image older women were presented with in myths and fairy tales, I swam every day, rode horseback, and was on a dark green veggie-juice diet. I was not entirely something out of Grimm's fairy tales. Nevertheless, the role of mothers in myth (and now for me in reality), which seemed to be standing on the sidelines wringing our hands watching the lives of grown children unfold, seemed unavoidable.

Anticlea got very little time in the imagination of the patriarchs. In *The Odyssey*, she has died—but not of old age or illness. It is speculated by some that she took her own life after being told the lie that her son was dead. I sympathized.

There were instances during that period when patriarchy no less affected me. To begin with, when a child fails, at any stage, in any way, eyes turn to the mother. The chorus (certain family members, immediate community, society in general), with few exceptions, appeared to point fingers at me as if to demand my banishment. After all, to me had been left the duty to produce a king or a hero. I imagined the whispers—*What more could anyone expect from a woman who left a husband and who, furthermore, behaved as if she had no use for men? How dare she think she could walk about and be as liberated as any man? No wonder her son turned out such a disappointment. What male role model had he had?* These toxic thoughts echoed in my skull the whole of his incarceration. When I wasn't sensing that others blamed me, I blamed myself.

When I'd finally go to bed, I'd select any number of books on the nightstand. Mi'jo had asked me to send him some of Bukowski's poetry. Remembering how much I had enjoyed Bukowski's work years before, I ordered his fiction for myself. Apparently, the poet had been asked by his small publisher to write a novel. The publisher believed in him and pledged a small sum to keep the writer going. Bukowski, famous for his lack of inhibition, enjoyment of constant inebriation, and unpretentiousness in all respects, did not find the transition daunting and proceeded to put out one novel after the next. The books were entertaining and not without their own truth.

One night, I thought I'd try my hand at a writing exercise

à la Bukowski. From the recesses of my writer's consciousness, I recalled certain writers of the twentieth century that I had enjoyed for their transgressive works. There was Georges Bataille, the philosopher who wrote about such topics as human sacrifice, necrophilia, and incest. One had to admire the French; they were not afraid to write the taboo. Bukowski wrote a story about a pedophile from the pedophile's perspective. The piece made me stop reading Bukowski—I didn't have room in my mind to entertain brutality to the indefensible. Still, as a self-taught writer, I learn from good literature even if the themes are not to my liking. I discovered I was on my way to writing a new book.

The following Valentine's Day, Mi'jo was released.

Today my solitude is a solid presence, as it has been for years. I've survived long enough, however, to accept love in all its variations.

Mariana at age 6 (Chicago; 2014).

Searching the Other Side

"Why do you believe in God?" my six-and-a-half-year-old granddaughter asked me one afternoon last year. It was a question that came out of the blue. I had not seen her since her sixth birthday when I was last in town. There is a lot of growing in a child's mind in six months. We had never talked about God.

"Well," I said, thinking out loud, "I believe in God because of all the glorious things in nature, the little birds and beautiful flowers and trees, snow in winter, and how the rain makes everything smell in spring . . ." Pajaritos, arbolitos, I said—using the diminutive, the indigenous way to speak of what we admire and enjoy. It shows our affection. I was still groping for an answer when she said curtly, "My mami and I don't believe in God."

"Oh," I replied.

Later, I mentioned it to Mi'jito.

"I felt like she and I were in the middle of a conversation," I told him. We had been having lunch in a Thai diner; she brought it up when I took her to the restroom. Maybe she was taking a survey because the subject of God came up here and there and, yet, her mother had told her to dismiss it.

When my son and Mariana's mami were together, neither seemed to be interested in any kind of religious practice. Believing in God, one could argue, is not the same thing as accepting the dogma of any institution. It made me wonder. If you weren't handed instructions as a child, as I was in catechism class, how would you come to have an understanding of "God" as a concept, if not a deity?

"Who is God?"

"God is the creator of heaven and earth, and of all things."

"Where is God?"

"God is everywhere."

"Why did God make you?"

"God made me to know Him, to love Him, and to serve Him in this world and be happy with him forever in heaven."

The Mexican nuns taught us children these first lessons in catechism class when I was my granddaughter's age. I made my First Holy Communion at seven. It was considered the age of reason, when you knew the difference between good and bad (maybe). What convinced me to memorize the answers correctly was that I would be made to spend time on my bare knees kneeling before the pietà in the classroom if I didn't.

Now we know (or at least, some of us would concur) that

just above the blue skies there is no Zeus figure sitting on a throne atop a cumulus. We've looked. At least as far as the moon and stars, so far no sign of him. Maybe people always knew it was a story, a fable, a metaphor, a way of making the masses understand there were big consequences for our actions. I'm not a theologian. However, it's always been my nature to try to understand, well, everything. Some matters, like the existence of a higher power, take a lifetime to answer for oneself. At least, this seems to be the case for me.

M'ijo had not much more to say on the subject. He had come around to the decision that felt to me as culturally relevant as it might be about faith. He decided to expose his daughter to the idea of an invisible God, a revolutionary spiritual figure named Jesus and his loving mother, Mary. Mary took the form of the Virgin of Guadalupe. There would be no Sunday school or official subscribing to the dogma of any religion, but when we three were together, we might even go to mass.

Speaking for myself, I couldn't testify for Jesus or an invisible God, but I put my feet to the fire for Our Lady of Guadelupe.

Octavio Paz once wrote that Mexicans believed in two things, the lottery and the Virgin of Guadalupe. Without question, the Madonna pervaded our culture. You don't have to be Catholic to have faith in her powers. People of Mexican heritage bear witness to her everywhere. In the United States, sightings on knots in oak trees, water stains on concrete under freeways, and reflections on the windows of business buildings testify to that fact. I don't know if it is human nature to be superstitious, or why long after we've come to know the causes of natural catastrophes, we still pray for protection against them. But whatever the reason, Mexicans are loyal to Guadalupe.

Since early on I had respect and love for the Mother of Jesus, the version whose blue mantle had turned green to go with the Mexican flag. My mother was a devotee. At twelve years old, she took me on my first pilgrimage to the basilica in Mexico City. I recall my aunt making her way on raw knees across the plaza and into the old church. During the mid-1970s, as I began to develop my political identity as a Chicana I also turned to honoring La Virgen de Guadalupe as my Imago Dei.

In La Virgen de Guadalupe was spiritual cache with which I could identify as a woman. In México among the indigenous peoples she was also called Tonantzin, who was a goddess revered in the Aztec (Mexica) Empire. I came to accept Our Lady of Guadalupe, whom I loved (and yet saw as stripped of goddess powers), as simultaneously the Great Mother, fecund and formidable. One of the characteristics of a goddess is to reign over some territory. Guadalupe Tonantzin reigns over México, or more precisely, Mexicans. She led the war for independence against Spain and the United Farmworkers movement of César Chávez in the United States.

I was brought up Catholic, but as I think back on it my parents were what we now refer to as "culturally Catholic." At home neither of my parents spoke to me about God. Yet, the solution to all problems according to my mother was for me to turn to Him to assist me. My father stayed silent on the subject until on his deathbed, when he asked me to go to mass with my mother and pray for his survival. (An appearance in church for me was rare but, of course, I went.) He did not want to die. My paternal grandmother, my primary caretaker, had converted to Protestantism. Still, she believed in La Virgen María, intermediary between us and God. Above all, she was a great believer in the supreme power of God, which she called upon for her work as a curandera.

Curanderas traditionally have basic areas of expertise. They may be yerberas—proficient in herbal medicine. They may work as sobadoras—or masseuses—but sobadoras also reset bones. Curanderas can be parteras; midwives were usually outside urban areas, especially in times past. The curanderas may also do some form of psychic work. She (or he) would be a vidente or seer. Having a don, or gift, is a term applied to all healers. These categories are not mutually exclusive. The psychic work is not for everybody, but a curandera would convey messages passed on from the Other Side and curanderas attribute any of their gifts to God, Tata Dios, El Mero Mero.

While her mother and other grandparents shared the conviction that there was no God, my granddaughter was firmly convinced by them that Santa Claus was real. Her fervent defense of the magical man's existence was understood not just by the proof of toys she received from him but her astute powers of deduction. If she stopped believing in the benevolent stranger, the gifts would stop coming. Moreover, if Santa Claus did not exist, who ate the milk and cookies left for his midnight visit?

The same rationale applied to the tooth fairy. Growing up on the immense popularity of Disney films, my nietecita had a clear idea of what the tooth fairy looked like: Tinkerbell. Tinkerbell was doe-eyed, bright as a lightning bug, and, therefore, real. God, on the other hand, was a no-show.

I would have taken the pretty and effervescent tooth fairy over the somber, invisible guardian angel catechism class taught me I had. My guardian angel didn't give me money, either. According to the nuns he was old, serious, and as silent as the air after the rains. Nevertheless, I do remember loving my guardian angel dearly for a time because he was there to protect me and I felt safe. I prayed to him every night. When I was away from home, I made room for him (or her?) next to me.

We were out and about one Sunday on a June afternoon. The whole world seems to be out during good weather in Chicago and we were no exception. My nieta had just lost a tooth and was saving it to put under her pillow that night. Her mother had promised the tooth fairy would leave her some money for it. I decided to play devil's advocate on the subject of the existence of God. I said, "Mi reina, you cannot believe in the tooth fairy if you don't believe in God."

"Why?" she asked in that way children do when having profound exchanges with adults, pretending to be distracted, playing, and bouncing about. All the while she was formulating new questions.

"Because," I said, "God created everything. He created the tooth fairy, too." She continued to play for a few minutes while I pondered why I would put something in my dear grandchild's head that I doubted myself.

I wasn't sure if I was trying to persuade her *against* believing in preposterous creatures like the tooth fairy and Santa Claus, against the notion of *going along* with such preposterous ideas for the sake of personal gain (money and toys), or, if I really did believe in the logic I was presenting. As I waded the murky waters of the unsure, I began to wonder if a special place would be waiting for me in hell if I did not give God some new thought.

My granddaughter, still actively moving around me with an Isadora Duncan spin here and there, was thinking it over. Then she asked, "Is it okay if I don't believe what Mami believes?"

"You are free to believe anything you want to believe," I said, perhaps too excitedly. Then, to my consternation, I found myself reverting to my own catechism lessons when I was around her age and said, "God gives us all free will."

The nuns had obviously done a very thorough job of programming my brain. Unlike when I was a child, my granddaughter saw not believing in God as a choice. Despite all my own conflicts about the existence of God, I was upset that she didn't have any foundation of belief to eventually build on or reject. How to keep her from becoming a full-fledged nihilist?

I set about contemplating God in order to have something coherent to offer my granddaughter. My own relationship with the concept of God had not been without long periods of doubt. When I was all grown-up, resolute about no longer being a practicing Catholic, I disassociated myself from the Catholic Church, which I saw as ridden with dogma so conflicting for me, especially as a woman. Years passed.

When I married, my new mother-in-law reintroduced angels into my life. La suegra had a complex, self-styled, and lively belief system. She had traveled from South America as a single woman with her only child in utero and had apprenticed in San Francisco with a Puerto Rican santero. Despite the lack of family, education, or the English language, she did fairly well in real estate. She believed in angels who turned themselves into human form to help us. An entire corner of her living room was dedicated to an altar of sorts. (Noticeably, there were numerous Madonna with the Holy Infant statues.) She prayed to a Native American chief spirit for luck and to a laughing Buddha for financial prosperity.

There were all kinds of statues, icons, glasses of clear water, offerings, and incense for burning.

From my observations of those who practice sympathetic magic, which is how I interpret to some degree such complex practices, you do not stay loyal to a spirit or saint who does not work for you. In my experience with such practitioners, however, ultimately, they attribute all mercies and blessings to God. Very often, their view of God is the ancient one as an all-powerful patriarch.

According to my suegra, there were spirit guides that involved themselves in human affairs. She was also a follower of the nineteenth-century author Allan Kardec, considered the founder of spiritism. Because of la suegra I read his books. The spiritism movement became very popular in the late nineteenth century and early twentieth century.

Another popular spiritist figure, and not in la suegra's sphere (but I mention for my own reasons), was Madame Blavatsky, cofounder of the Theosophical Society. Blavatsky traveled to Tibet and the Middle East. She believed that all religions stemmed from an ancient wisdom in reincarnation. Spirits, for Blavatsky, were not our dead speaking to us but other beings who existed between the living and the dead. While my suegra never heard of Blavatsky, she subscribed to a similar acceptance of otherworldly entities among us.

After the passing of my suegra's mentor, the santero, she

continued to hold séances every Friday night in her home. This I know because shortly after we had all met, the santero and my mother-in-law recruited me to contact the spirits for them. They had both decided that I had the gift to be a medium.

Mediums are very essential to the practice of spiritism or spiritualism; the difference for the early developers of these beliefs sometimes overlaps. No one else was invited to the Friday-night sessions when I was around and received instruction. My husband never participated. Throughout our five-year marriage he preferred other activities, such as the materialist struggle of the masses (but not exclusively, as eventually the word that he had girlfriends came back to me). His frequent absences, I'm sure, led me to go along at first with the séances because otherwise I'd have been alone and bored. My loneliness in our marriage came early on because when he wasn't putting in long hours as a welder, he dedicated his time to the workers' overthrow of the bourgeoisie or trying to revive grassroots organizations that had been hit hard during the Reagan administration that we were living under. At home, he stayed up late into the night writing what I could only imagine was some form of manifesto. He was as invested in the people's needs as his mother was concerned with our transcendental security.

I found myself answering la suegra's requests to act as her conduit between the material world and the one beyond. They could ask me anything and I would answer.

Sometimes, if the messages were particularly heartrending, I wept. Until I learned to remove anything metal, rings or bracelets, I'd end up with my flesh burned from them, as one would expect would happen to a conduit transmitting electromagnetic currents.

My suegra and the santero had explained that electric currents were all around and were how spirits channeled their messages through to our side. If you placed a clear glass of water on the table to direct yourself to a spirit, a profusion of bubbles would soon rise. This was the spirit making itself known. You would always keep a clear glass of water somewhere near the door to absorb bad spirits that tried to enter with any visitor, they advised.

I learned a lot about the Other Side and all the invisible beings that meddled in our lives through my turban-wearing mother-in-law. On one occasion when I was expecting my son, my suegra called me to her garden. Handing me a strap, she then blindfolded me and instructed that I beat a rosebush that had refused to bloom. My suegra believed that the rosebush would become fertile under the reprimand of a fertile woman. It would only work with a woman who was having her first child. (Okay, it didn't sound credible, but out of respect I went along and beat the poor bush.) Come spring, just as la suegra said her spirit guides had assured her, the rosebush bloomed.

I learned how to communicate with the invisible world and did not forget after my marriage ended. However, as time went on I found it less important in my life. There were simply too many questions as to whether or not invisible entities, from guardian angels to bad spirits, accompanied all our acts.

Secondly, despite my apparent knack for it, I sometimes doubted my ability to channel spirits. Was it possible that I was not a medium but a psychic who picked up thoughts and just fed it all back? In any case, the one and only ultimate source la suegra taught me to thank for any don was God.

Over a dozen years later, the practice of being a medium came back to me via another direction. The summer that my mother passed away I was invited by friends to come stay with them in México and heal from the loss. One day, my hostess and I went to visit a well-known indigenous medicine man in a village near Tepoztlán. The energy of Tepoztlán attracts a wide range of new-age followers. There is a small temple atop a hill from the late classical period that is a challenge to climb. Anyone looking for a curandera, a spiritual cleansing, or alternative herbal medicine may find it in that town. Some claim they've seen ominis, or spaceships, circling above the hilltops. Tepoztlán's reputation goes back to before the conquest. Practitioners of the black arts were said to be found there, while in the adjacent village of Amatlán, you could find healers of good intentions.

Don Lupe, I'll call him, was from Tlaxcala and in his

seventies when we met. Spanish was his second language and Don Lupe was both a curandero of the traditional kind (doing spiritual cleansings on people or their properties) and a granicero. Before the conquest, the graniceros were the keepers of the rains and in charge of appeasing the gods to assure good harvests. My friend Penélope had been initiated by Don Lupe to be a granicera. Penélope was not indigenous. She came from a distinguished Euro-Mexican family and, long ago, her father had nearly become president of México.

Don Lupe never spoke to me directly. Instead, as if she needed to translate, he would relay to Penélope whatever "messages" from the gods or his ancestors he was getting about me. She would translate to English although she knew I'd understood him clearly. (The view that Mexicans have of gringos isn't always about ethnicity; I was still a Yankee, after all.) Like la suegra, Don Lupe kept a myriad of objects on a long table he used as an altar, and he also seemed to lean toward Catholicism but was open to many religious icons.

Without judgment I viewed his altar, but when he insisted that we all purchase a certain kind of amulet for protection from him, I had a problem with the obligatory and substantial fee. After much reflection, however, I decided Don Lupe was sincere about believing I needed protection and I obtained it. I've not forgotten the night we dropped in on Don Lupe unexpectedly. It was a thunderous night full of lightning everywhere. We found him outside burning incense over a fogón, an outdoor fire.

"There is much opposition to her in the world," he said to my friend about me. "She needs our protection." He had gone pale imagining the world I moved around in, the world that had all but annihilated our indigenous way of being.

Amulets are not as far-fetched as we'd like to think. Every one of us, it seems, holds some form of superstition. The battle against the wicked is universal. Until it came apart, my granddaughter wore a red string around her wrist, which her atheist mother had instructed she not remove. Now that she had turned seven, I wanted to explain to her that if one did not believe that a force such as God (good) existed then neither could evil. It was possible that no other adult had spoken to her about the principle of duality that permeated Western civilization. Many of us performed small rituals for good luck. Who was watching over us? The universe? In my opinion, it was a semantic replacement for "God."

One time I asked Don Lupe if he would allow me to come and apprentice with him. As far as I could see, he performed many of the cleansing rituals that Mexican curanderos were known for, the use of the egg, herbs, and, of course, their own abilities to mediate for us with the gods or the spirit world. The folks that came to him for these cleansing rituals ranged from humble indigenous to new-age whites to comfortable or wealthy nationals or foreigners. Don Lupe was adamant that he had nothing to teach me. He said I had come to the world equipped with teachings.

When the medicine man was young he was struck by lightning, which put him in a coma. During that time he claimed he'd dwelled in heaven and there he met a beautiful lady in a red dress. Upon his return to consciousness he discovered that lady was Santa Barbara. Santa Barbara was the entity Don Lupe most appealed to for his healing. He recommended that in my new role as granicera as well as curandera I should solicit the guidance of Santa Barbara, too. He could not tell me what my work would be because in my current incarnation, he had "seen" that I was far more advanced than most of the healers around. In fact, he proclaimed that I chose to return to this life to be a director of those who came to "heal." They would be active in their incarnations as teachers, psychologists, or in spiritual-healing practices, like Reiki and other bodywork.

I returned to Tepoztlán over many years. One year, Penélope asked the old man why I wasn't made to make the yearly trek up the volcano with all the rest. She meant the annual ceremonies of the graniceros who took a pilgrimage up to a cave of the volcano of Iztaccíhuatl. All mounds, great and small, were considered gods by my indigenous ancestors. They sometimes took the form of humans. The stories of the volcanoes and the low mountains of México go back to preconquest times and are rich with accounts of romances filled with jealousies and breakups. It explains why some are located where they are and take the shapes that they do. Syncretism is part of the modern indigenous belief system. Don Lupe did not think it necessary for me to join them.

"She doesn't have to!" he shouted, not so much to emphasize but because of his own partial deafness, caused by the lightening incident. "I've seen her. Going here and there. She is doing her work. She is doing what she is supposed to be doing! She goes to those who need her." His crooked index finger motioned throughout the air as if to indicate that I was flying. When he said he "saw" me he pointed to his eye. He did not mean he *saw* me but instead with the third eye perhaps, or another way. Later, Penélope explained to me that Don Lupe took the red seeds of a plant to "see."

The idea that because a spiritual gift was granted by God (or deities or saints) people should flatly not profit from the services, in my opinion, ought to be qualified. What I learned from all of the curanderos I engaged with in México, including Don Lupe, is that they all felt they had a right to charge or accept donations. After all, everyone had to eat. No doubt there were many scam artists among the Mexican curanderos and esoteric practitioners. One example that stands out was in Tepoztlán. It was a part-time curandero, recommended to me by his mother, a curandera and yerbera. She was old, spry, and ran a temazcal. In ancient times the temazcal served as a kind of steam cleansing bath and remained a Mexican spiritual practice. Yerberas worked with herbal medicine and in Tepoztlán many were certified by the government. They had a genuine knowledge and understanding of the herbal products they employed and sold.

I went with Alba, a granicera and curandera whom I'd met through Don Lupe, to see the young curandero. We decided to test him. Alba was to have the consultation. The young curandero told me and the granicera that his spirit guide was Bruce Lee. Standing on his dirt-floored consultorio off the plaza, we ended up refusing to give him the sum he outright charged. It was fifty dollars, a lot of money for an average local curandera, mi amiga, to pay for a consultation. Certainly my friend couldn't afford it. No doubt he considered the gringa (me) had it. His mother had perhaps filled him in on my background. During carnival in Tepoztlán I ran into him again near the market. In addition to the curandero hustle, he was a cop. He, and his protector Bruce Lee, ignored me.

Not all of my spiritual entreaties were in vain. Repeatedly, I was told that the spirit Santa Barbara or Changó (or Shangó or Xangô) was with me. Santa Barbara's reappearance took me back to la suegra's beliefs in Santería. The androgynous deity-saint was among the most powerful figures recognized along the Caribbean coast. During the Inquisition, slaves and subsequent followers of the Yoruba religion disguised their deities as Catholic saints for safety purposes. My suegra had a statue of Santa Barbara on her altar, which she most likely came to know through the Puerto Rican santero.

Santa Barbara and Changó came to me yet another time some years later, during a trip to Cuba on an informal visit with friends. Two of the teachers with me took toys and supplies to a school they had contacted in advance. The Writers' Union of Cuba asked me for modems for the Internet connections that were used then, as well as other supplies. We brought new T-shirts and clothes in all sizes. One of the women I met at the union offices was able to wear some of the clothes and came to thank me personally.

Days later, the same woman walked excitedly toward me and shouted, "You are a daughter of Changó!" She then informed me that she was a Yoruba priestess and invited me to her home. The purpose was to present me with the necklace of Changó. I didn't then nor do I now know much about the Yoruba religion or the Santería practices of Cuba. The priestess, called Fe, gave me her address and I promised to see her at an appointed time.

That day, bright and clear, I caught a bicitaxi to Fe's home. Off we went, my stealth cabbie peddling along the Malecón, sea breeze in my hair and against my face. I had no idea where I was going or what the process of receiving Changó's necklace would entail. It ended up being a quick, loving, and private encounter. Having no association with the religion, I took it as an honor. I imagined the blessing she bestowed was her own way of offering gratitude. I don't remember if she clarified why she decided I was a daughter of Changó, but my belief was that she received this message from the orichas.

While we may dismiss the stories of pots breaking in the skies that explain thunder or the sparks of a god's arrows that provoke lightning, we ought not dismiss what we know through the sciences. As a Chicana (a label one deliberately gives herself for political reasons and these kinds of affirming culture ties), it has been important to me to revive traditions from before the devastation incurred on the indigenous psyche by the conquest.

My little statue and necklace remain on my altar in an adobe capilla I built a decade ago in the desert of New Mexico. It is dedicated to Our Lady of Guadalupe. With all due respect to the practices and beliefs of those whose paths crossed with mine in México, Cuba, and elsewhere, certain objects on my altar are now mementos. They are not mementos like glass globes that you set on the mantel for show. They are benchmarks of my spiritual journey.

My own journey involving curandera practices, God, the saints, Our Lady of Guadalupe, and being Mexican (but not necessarily Catholic) go back to my grandmother, who was the neighborhood curandera. It was a vibrant, newly growing Mexican community. The old woman, as ancient and wise as something out of a Gabriel García Márquez story, was my primary caretaker until her passing when I was going on ten years old. She kept cans of medicinal herbs all around, gave massages to visitors who came in and out of our flat to get help, and had boundless heart, especially with children. All of this made life-lasting impressions on me.

However, the most significant gift that my grandmother

brought into my life was unconditional love. It is because of that old woman's presence in my formative years that I learned compassion for others and had it for myself when I've needed it most. It is my conviction that without at least one such figure in a child's life, who shows trust and caring as an example to follow, the child will grow up lost in society. It is because of my abuelita who signed her relief check with an X that I am convinced I was able to be a mother and, even, the writer that I became. Her example in giving unconditional love, not just to me, but to all who were around her, made me forever grateful.

Ultimately, what I came away with from the curanderos (the sincere ones, at least) is that they were all motivated by the same principle: that offering care to other beings nourishes one's inner self. The Buddhists believe that through our many incarnations we have all been mothers in one life or another. It is the mother's caring nature that we should aspire to emulate. In today's world, mother is the one who protects, witnesses, nourishes, and nurtures with unreserved compassion.

"What do you need?" Our Lady of Guadalupe Tonantzin asked St. Juan Diego Speaking Eagle. "Am I not here, your mother?" She addressed him as her son but he, a learned man, was not a boy. He addressed her, in turn, in the affectionate way the indigenous address loved ones, using diminutives and endearments. He called her "mi niña." It refers to a girl, but the term is also used for someone we hold precious and wish to please.

Feminine power came to me as a child in the form of Our Lady of Guadalupe. I connect with her culturally as well as spiritually. From the first parish I attended in Chicago to when I found myself in Notre Dame on the Left Bank of Paris to strolling over the ancient marble stones at Ephesus in Turkey, she has been there to meet me. The Council of Ephesus was where the Christian church fathers restored her name to "Mother of God," as the ancients called their goddesses before. Not far from Ephesus, I visited the house where Mary went to live after Jesus was crucified. Seeing Guadalupe Tonantzin in different places connects me to my ancestry and with the world. In México, she was not the only aspect of Mary that appeared in the Americas, but she demonstrated her fortitude and stamina by becoming the most popular.

The Virgin Mary was not the Great Mother, as Jung described, both solicitous and devouring. Instead, the Catholic Church reduced the Mother of Jesus into a passive figure. She may be appealed to, but she was a middleman; she reigned over nothing. The Great Mother in México might have been interchangeably the goddess of Coatlicue and of Tonantzin. For a long time among the indigenous especially, those goddesses remained synonymous with Our Lady of Guadalupe, who had appeared on the hill called Tepeyac.

The goddesses of the Aztec-Mexica people, on the other hand, did include within themselves oppositional energies.

Beyond a topic of academic investigation, Chicanas do overwhelmingly believe in the goddess. We believe in her in the same way as perhaps many believe in God today. She is not a spirit in a woman's body floating around and eaves-dropping to see how our day is going and ready to respond to every solicitation for help. She will not forsake us if we were not deserving. Instead, she represents a force that we may call upon from deep within ourselves to remember our own courage. We do it in different ways. Some solicit her through spontaneous prayers or by reciting the Rosary. Some go to church to attend mass or speak to a priest. Others keep an altar at home and light candles just as, in various ways, Christians perform rituals to assure themselves of Father God's omnipresence.

My own hyperdulia for Our Lady of Guadalupe led me to erect a chapel on my desert land in her name. It was hand built using adobes made from mud and straw, circular, and what I consider Zen in its minimalism. The only icon is a five-feet-tall custom-designed stained-glass image of Our Lady of Guadalupe. It faces east and welcomes the light of dawn in each new day.

As my granddaughter was about to turn seven, I found myself at mass with her. I showed her how to make the sign of the Cross. Even as I muttered the words "In the name of the Father, the Son, and Holy Ghost," I became critically aware of the male dominance in that gesture. Internally, I criticized my instruction. Why was I sending the message to a female child of the twenty-first century that she didn't exist in the divine equation?

I gave it deep thought. Soon, I came to understand a modest and, to be sure, highly personal interpretation of early lessons in Catholicism. I told my nieta how I saw the triune view of God: we *all* were the Father, Son, and Holy Ghost. We use three fingers (also representative of the Trinity) and start at the forehead (presumably where the middle eye is located) and commend ourselves to the "Father"—"Father" or "Lord" for the ancients represented "knowing." It meant our consciousness.

Next, we point to the solar plexus or, perhaps, the heart, and say "the Son." The Son was God made flesh. The Son, Jesus, was the body our conscious mind inhabited.

Tapping the left then the right shoulder, we commend ourselves to the Holy Spirit. The Holy Spirit was action. It was our breath and inspiration. In this way we commend ourselves to God—or, simply, to the good.

My interpretation might be seen as having nothing to do with Catholic doctrine. Some might say that teaching my granddaughter to see God in herself and to love her fiercely (to paraphrase Ntozake Shange) is blasphemous.

I can live with that.

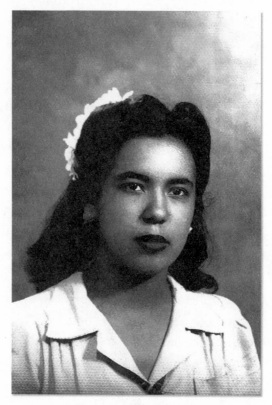

Mamá, age 14 (Mexico City; 1941).

Black Dove

Paloma negra, paloma negra,
¿dónde,dónde andarás?
Ya no sé si maldecirte o por ti rezar.

—"Paloma Negra"

When Mi'jo was eight, I accepted a teaching residency for a semester at Mills College in Oakland, California. In the early nineties, the elitist vestiges of the women's school of higher education were evident. I was given an apartment in a cocoon of a campus splashed with green hills and draping eucalyptus trees. Coeds did laps in an outdoor pool where the climate was prime all year round.

At Mills, a young man, Guillermo, befriended me. He was one of the few graduate males on campus, a kind of scruffy-artist type. I ignored several attempts on his part to say hello. It wasn't until he called out to me in Spanish one day that I stopped and noticed him. He was from Mexico City and was preparing to start an MFA in music. Mills's music program was known for adhering to John Cage's modernist theories; this attracted the young Guillermo, and it was at Mills that he met a pianist who became his girlfriend and, later, wife. He and I hit it off. One day he told me he was preparing an experimental chamber performance in my honor. The music school was going to produce it.

This was a big deal for all involved. Guillermo's mother and aunt flew in from Mexico City. My mamá, by chance, was visiting from Chicago.

If I recall the evening with images based on feelings, I might picture the young maestro's mother and aunt in large plumed hats and fox furs à la Posada in the days of Porfirio Díaz. True to my mother's definition of me, I see myself as a bohemian. Having by then made my home in New Mexico, I am wearing cowboy boots and a vintage Mexican skirt fit for the Mabel Dodge Luhan clique. How did my mother appear that evening? I roll myself into a ball like an armadillo and allow myself to think of her. Like the armadillo that fends off attacks, I feel I must somehow protect us.

A stoic woman always, she was showing signs of frailty, inside and out. My mamá wore black and, maybe, a vinyl coat from someplace like Burlington Coat Factory. Save for a stroke of dark red or orange lipstick, no makeup. She dyed her hair black at home over the laundry tub in the basement to avoid messing the house. The amateur job made it brassy orange in places, and white roots jutted out almost immediately. In the last decade of her life, in her sixties, she wore a kind of basic, short cut, like you might get at a barbershop.

Mamá didn't go to beauty shops and never polished her nails, not even to disguise the thumbnail puncture through the bone from when a drill press had seared through it. My mamá's foreman sent her home for the day. That was it. She went back to work the next day, back to the drill press. No thought of a lawsuit or to bring awareness of the unsafe conditions. I don't know what my father (who worked as a drill-press operator) thought of the accident, but I do remember one time when I was around eleven or so, he came home shaken. A young Puerto Rican woman at his factory had lost four fingers in a clean swoop. It was before guardrails on such rapid machinery. No doubt, like my mother, not much was done after initial medical care. It's hard to believe now, but my mother was relieved not to be fired.

Mamá now had diabetes and, while never fat to start with, she had reduced down to a small pellet of a woman. She always had nice teeth but lost one on the top right, which caused her to cover her mouth with a hand when she spoke. The picture I'm giving is of a somber woman, but my mother had a loud wide-open-mouth laugh before losing that tooth. *HA-HA-HA!* she'd crack up, until tears ran down. In public, however, it was more likely that she didn't just put a hand up but stifled the laugh altogether. I admire people who can laugh out loud. I have my father's way of receiving something we find funny, a side grin or a chuckle. It is possible people don't inherit laughs.

But back to my mamá; she was not without her charms. She enjoyed dancing with a partner and although it was uncommon to see, she and my father cut a rug nicely with danzón, cha-cha, and mambo steps. It was her voice that I most often remember with nostalgia. I see her in very few images—a silhouette in my mind dancing in a 1950s dress that accentuated her short but shapely figure. As if I'd saved a digital recording, I can still hear her perfect pitch, her voice like almond-infused tequila, deep and mellow.

When I was a small child, playing quietly on my own while my mamá prepared a perfect Mexican-style rice from scratch (in the days before Osterizers became commonplace and one used a molcajete to grind tomatoes, garlic, onion, and cumin), she sang or whistled to popular Spanish tunes that played on the radio.

As a singer, she was not exactly an amateur. As teenagers when they lived at the border, Mamá and her siblings sang live on the radio. It was during World War II and the Andrews Sisters were boogie-woogie-ing with the bugle boy, and gringo soldiers who crossed over to Laredo had Georgia on their minds.

"I knew the words to all the songs," she told me when I was growing up and sat with her in the kitchen preparing beans for long hours of boiling, or in her bedroom as she'd fold freshly ironed clothes to store in drawers. "But like a parrot, I just mimicked what I heard, not knowing what I was saying," she laughed. *You always hurt the one you love . . .* There was vibrato in her voice, the kind for which we who couldn't sing yearned.

She never spoke to me in English. Mamá taught me not just Spanish but indigenous words, which she may have learned from the grandfather who raised her. On that marriage bed of hers, surely the one on which I was conceived, I loved to hear all her stories. When I was ten my father took the night shift and I got to sleep with her. She showed me how to sleep cucharita fashion—to spoon—and I slept the slumber of the angels in my mamá's arms. I made her laugh to tears trying to pronounce the "tl" in Náhuatl—ichpochtli (muchacha), tototl (bird), nantli (mamá). I grew up believing that singing and whistling on pitch were talents possessed by all mothers. When I became a mother I also sang "A la ru-ru niño" to my baby, softly, with no vibrato, but remembering how Mamá always soothed me.

The evening of the chamber performance, the reception was cramped; I recall a stifling crowd. Mamá obviously felt out of place, lonely, ill at ease. She seemed tiny; people standing in front of her obstructed our view from each other. She went, as perhaps she hoped, unnoticed. There, that evening, she had all but disappeared, my mamá.

Diabetes was taking her slowly. Not long before, she had lost her lifelong companion, my father, the man who danced with her and helped her make a home in Chicago. Who knows what she was feeling among strangers at that reception? How aware was she of the things I think of now, straining to understand her awkward discomfort?

Las gran señoras from Mexico City and I were introduced. Most likely they were not in plumed hats but sporting stylish hairstyles, and I may well have left the boots at home for a pair of chic shoes to go with a short dress and big earrings on that occasion. I don't know if I impressed them much as the inspiration for Guillermo's music. I don't recall the conversation, if any. We certainly made no lunch plans. I looked around for my mamá so as to introduce her. She was sitting not far.

She always enjoyed food, and the image of her there, shyly tasting the hors d'oeuvres, is clear. I gave her a signal. I called softly, "Ma." Her look was stern, something like fear in her hooded eyes, the whites moist, red. "Ma?" Shaking an index finger at me that said no, she refused. Without her suddenly, without anyone at my side—but especially without her, the woman who bore me, who made me to be—I felt alone there. She was the only woman permitted to scold me or whose praises mattered to me. At home my mamá expressed her opinions, criticisms, and occasional compliments. I took it all in. With regards to my mother, love and connection were synonymous. Throughout my life I yearned for that tie with her, and often I did not feel it. No doubt, it provoked me to be the mother I became—more open. Present. Past comfort zones.

My mother didn't want anything to do with these fancy people. It didn't matter that they were from Mexico City, the same place where she was raised. It didn't matter that they spoke Spanish, the language she was comfortable speaking. They were white and not in the same worlds. I could have reached over right then and done what I have not been able to do in the nearly two decades since her death, grab her veiny hands and hold them close to my cheeks. But I didn't.

Mills College wasn't the first place my mother recoiled; it was in any public space. She'd never gone to school meetings. She hardly socialized outside of her immediate family. When I was a child we took buses to the movies, to the Teatro Zenith to see live galas with Agustín Lara or María Victoria, or even went far out to the Forest Preserves to attend Mexican Sunday picnics. A polka band played at these, but she never danced or spoke to anyone. The only things I know she did on her own were to go to work at the factory, run errands, and visit close family.

When I was a teenager and she no longer felt it necessary to have me along, my father (who by then had a car) drove her anywhere she wanted to go. No one *needed* to translate for her anymore in places like the doctor's office, but she still preferred others to speak for her. Where there were Mexicans my mamá was more confident but not particularly social. She always told her children that knowing English was the key to the kingdom.

English is native for me, but I nevertheless inherited much of her unease in public spaces. I, too, might shrink to a corner at gatherings, and when out and about I can't wait to return to the seclusion of my home. This is in contrast to my father, born in Chicago, a Robert De Niro look-alike. Tall and self-assured in a suit, he made his entrance in any room. "Cadillac Ray," my father. People always took him for white. Meanwhile, my indigenous mother, orphaned as a child, lived with an unshakable sense of displacement. She would have preferred to be a watermark on the wallpaper than bring even incidental attention to herself. This odd polarity between my parents formed my public and private personas.

The turbulent times of the late sixties and seventies shaped my way of thinking as much as my parents did. Civil rights leaders and a Democratic president had been assassinated in broad daylight by nefarious forces. Yet, the youth believed it was the government itself behind these shocking events. Latin America was run by dictatorships. We had Kent State and Vietnam. It was an unsafe time to be outspoken anywhere in the world.

I was in college studying art when I made the choice to pursue poetry and, later, prose. Writing and literature became my life and would be my own form of activism. Any idea of actually "studying" writing felt like potentially murky ground at best and dangerous at worse. If my experience in a writing class were to be anything like art classes had been, it would certainly be a risk. As a brown female—timid, too—I almost always felt overlooked or ignored outright. It was also a time when an ethnic slur by a teacher was acceptable and, if he were tenured, it was futile to complain. In art classes, male instructors were surrounded by male aspiring artists. White girls caught their eyes, too, even if their work did not.

Experience had taught me to be wary; I wrote on my own. On the plus side, I felt free to read and write as I pleased. I started teaching by happenstance in ethnic studies. By the eighties many of the Latino writers were also making their living through teaching while promoting a literature that had blossomed or, perhaps a better word, erupted out of cultural pride and political commitment.

The road ahead as a writer was likely to be paved with sheer force of will. There were black activists and writer stars, but US Latinos and Latinas were not being published in the mainstream. A few men—Piri Thomas in the sixties and, at the other extreme of thought and consciousness much later, the essayist Richard Rodriguez—became prominent. But Latinas were not yet considered.

By then I had both feet planted in feminist thought. Feminism as it might be applied to working-class women of color was untracked territory. My personal life and my writer's life became one. The man I married was a card-carrying Communist. The Marxist-Leninist and Chicana feminist household that we formed was not vying for entrance into any country club. He and I, stubborn in our convictions, kept things running at home and in our own writing and ideological activities.

By the nineties, visibility for Latinos and Latinas in the United States was progressing. Even if it was due mostly to expanding numbers, we were not as marginalized as we had once been. In my gut, I knew that one day the drawbridge to the great literary castle would come down and Latina writers could cross. Not all of us, of course, only those poised to dash over. In the economic system we lived in, it was not enough to be talented or work hard—you had to be ready. Considering how things were going in the country, I estimated it would take another ten years for the United States to embrace Chicana feminists. It turned out to be about eight. By then I was turning forty and I had been writing for twenty years. I was ready, all right.

As my work began to take clear form and direction, there was the question of my personal life. My factory-employed parents wondered when I would accept what people like us expected of the American Dream: a mortgage, children, a practical car, and paying your taxes on time. I thought they would be happy that I married at all, especially to someone much like them: a hardworking Latino. He did not have the lofty dreams of the "bohemian." We mortgaged a modest building in an inner-city neighborhood. I did part-time teaching to give myself time to also work on my writing.

He had children prior to our marriage and was in no rush to start a family together—but he wasn't opposed either. In the end, it was left to me. My age was a factor. By age forty, a woman took higher risks with a pregnancy. There was also the matter of finances. What compromises or sacrifices would an aspiring writer have to make as a mother? I could only imagine.

A few years later, I became a single mother and the dance of anxiety and compromise became constant. Finding full-time employment and affordable apartments, taking care of a child usually with no friends or family around, giving readings out of town, and writing at night were ongoing balls in the air. I lit a lot of candles during that time.

When I was flown to Mills from Albuquerque for the interview, I had no one with whom to leave my seven-year-old son and so I brought him along. His blue backpack was filled with schoolbooks, homework, and his X-Men and Ninja Turtles comics. During the required public talk I asked the department secretary to keep an eye on my little boy. Later, one of my Mills colleagues would say to me, "You know, Ana, we watched you with your little son, running all over campus. It was a deciding factor in bringing *you* to a women's college." They commended me for being a role model, but it was also simply my reality.

Mi'jo often had to travel with me to readings. When he became a teen, we moved to Chicago where there was my ailing mother at home and friends. He would gladly stay behind—by then he protested the interruptions in his routine brought on by my work trips.

While my life was unfolding in ways I hadn't planned, working mothers were familiar to me. Mamá supported the household. She always held a full-time factory job plus part-time jobs. She sold Avon beauty products for thirty-eight years, until her death. Before Avon worked out as a side gig, she tried a household product company and selling greeting cards. Until I was eight or nine, I accompanied her to people's homes on Saturdays. They were all in walking distance, or at least we always walked. I was to sit and say nothing. If they offered me anything to eat or drink, I was to say no. People were friendly and happy to get their family names on Christmas cards or order guaranteed cleaning products. They were Mexicans, new immigrants, eager to fit in. (When I was around ten, Mamá made an attempt to send me out on my own, a tiny Avon Lady going door to door. That effort didn't work for long; no one who opened her door was prepared to buy from a child who had no sales pitch.)

Saturday was bath day, so we often stumbled in on that ritual. In flats back then, you would still find apartments with no tubs and shared bathrooms. The canvas portable tub had been set out in the kitchen and the family members would take turns. Although vermin were no strangers in our own home, I've never gotten out of mind one visit to a young homemaker who sat on a cushioned chair across from my mother and me. The cushion was pushed up at the corner and a dead mouse lay underneath, seemingly staring up at me the whole time.

Mamá worked at one factory that made kitchen utensils way out in the suburbs. She had to take three buses every morning and three buses back home, after which she would prepare dinner. The last factory where she and my father both worked produced auto parts during peacetime and hand grenades during various "interventions." When that factory relocated to Southeast Asia in the eighties, both my parents were forced out of the job market, considered too old for unskilled labor that demanded quotas. This was the life my parents wanted to spare their children—no glory and no gratitude for contributing to the American Dream of the privileged. In honesty, they didn't expect great things for their future; they made do and hoped for better for their children.

After the split with my husband, I earned my income through speaking gigs, part-time teaching jobs, and college residencies. I was without mentors, sponsors, family support, or even a vague road map. My parents were caring and, in their own way, present. They did not know or understand their daughter, as a person, a woman, or a mother. "If you need anything, we're here," was how my father would end long-distance calls. Yet, if on the rare occasion I needed a loan or sought advice, he would turn the phone over to my mother who would promptly end the call. The separation with my husband left them confused. The hardworking guy was supposed to be my provider and protector for life. Now what?

"You change men like you change shoes," my father said to me once.

"Well, I do like shoes," I replied.

As for my mother, I confided to her about a crush I had on a professor I knew—a man who, in fact, used my books in his courses.

"Don't aim so high," she advised, though I had completed a PhD and had several books published by then.

My father was in his fifties when he died of lung cancer. My child was six. On his deathbed, perhaps grasping for some wisdom to impart, he rasped: "Don't take drugs." I almost looked around to see if he was talking to someone else. I'd never had any issues with drugs. I wonder if it simply came from the new slogan by the First Lady then, Nancy Reagan, which rang nonsensibly in the ears of Americans like the ice-cream truck going by: *Just say no to drugs, just say no to drugs*.

In the eighties, legal and illegal drugs gushed into the country. They flowed up and down economic channels and social strata. The cocaine I passed up at nightclubs or parties was still circulating when my son was coming up. Heroin offered to me in the seventies in the nice white California town where I first taught became as common as dirt in America. Crack, more popular than Coca-Cola on the streets, became crank and killed children of every color and creed. Meth was all over from big cities to exclusive suburbs to hick towns. I had "the talk" with Mi'jo early and often about the rules for our family of two.

La verdad: I feared for him whenever he walked out the door. In what neighborhood—town or city, rural area or village in the country—could I raise a brown boy and believe that no harm could ever come to him, where no drugs would appear? Where in the country would we live where no one—thug or cop—could ever point a gun at him? We had moved around the country as he was growing up and I did not believe that any high school, private or otherwise, would entirely and always promise to spare a brown boy of the violence brought on by drugs, gangs, or basic bullying of some sort. I sound negative, even alarmist, in admitting this, perhaps. Then again, maybe not. By the time he was in high school, metal detectors at school entranceways were taken for granted. The massacre in Columbine, one example that led to these practices nationwide, was neither in a metropolis nor considered populated by poor or "minority" students.

One evening when Mi'jo was seventeen, local TV reported that a young white man was shot sitting in a car with his brother in broad daylight. The shooting was in Evanston, an affluent suburb that is home to Northwestern University and the area where my son was headed that night. I called the police station and put my son on the phone to firmly remind him that Chicago had a curfew for minors. He hadn't done anything wrong, my son. He just wanted to go out on a Saturday night for a few hours. But I was in mother-anxiety mode. I feared for his life and well-being. I panicked that the pitfalls were too many for him to avoid each and every time. I kept him on my watch through college. And then, one day, my fears morphed into reality.

In public, from my understanding, men of color have to be wary and defensive. They posture physical strength. Mi'jo constructed his male persona from those involved in hip-hop—the rappers and artists he admired. Men of color learned to be men not necessarily from their loving or strong or vulnerable mothers at home but from other men and from their fathers, whether present or absent.

A long time ago, I came to interpret the story of Bambi in the enchanted forest as analogous to raising a male child and his rite of passage into manhood.

In the story, Bambi enjoys the nurturance and protection of his mamá, until one fateful day, as they peacefully enjoy a berry-and-leaf lunch, they are nearly overcome by the thunderous passing of a herd of stags. Bambi is both in awe and intimidated. "*Who* was that?" he asks his mother, nodding at the leader of the stags. "*That*," she reveals, "was your father." Ready to flex his own muscles, Bambi can't wait to join the herd. At this point, the mother's job in rearing the young is done. We all have to grow up sometime.

The rite of passage into masculine adulthood throughout history has been mostly about the preservation of the species, tribe, or nation. Males join forces to go off on the hunt or to battle together. They prepare with segregated dances and ayahuasca ceremonies and such. (No females and their bloody times allowed.) In the Bambi tale, however, in order to separate from his mother it isn't enough that the young male leave her. The mother must be obliterated so as to ensure that Bambi be released from the dangers of his mother's influence, preventing him from becoming a true buck. The young deer then assumes his legacy in the fierce male-dominated world.

Bambi's story has come back to me time and again when I think of my son. I chose to leave his father, who then decided we deserved no support. His father quickly moved on to other women, who had their own children with him. My son was always welcomed to join the new families his father formed, but he wanted no part of raising our son together. There were times when our child was growing up when my ex said or did things indicating he preferred to think I no longer existed. Our son, he had made his position clear, would receive no financial support from him unless he had full custody. So, I financially supported Mi'jo all the way through college. My son wished for intimacy with his father and, until high school, agreeably joined in with his father's new family, first one, then another, during school breaks. After the split, we never lived in the same state again. By the time Mi'jo reached high school, his response to his father's rejection was to reject right back—during those years, he did not always spend his vacations with his father's family. Still, he craved that relationship—yearned for it—I've come to realize.

Traditional thinking about gender roles is that we learn how to be women and mothers from our mothers and how to be men and fathers from our fathers. All that is changing, albeit slowly, in postmodern society, where gender roles are being scrutinized not just by feminists but by a whole new generation for whom gender is not viewed in such absolute terms.

If our goal is to spare children pitfalls and pain, whether single or in a two-parent household, it isn't possible. At times, even as we must avoid all of the sharks in deep waters, we, too, must become sharklike and move forward—lest we die.

Until the day Mamá passed, I was the daughter of my mamá for better or worse. It was a Saturday. While she was at the dialysis center getting treatment, I was back home cleaning the house. Two poet friends dropped by unexpectedly. They found me with a mop in hand. I was unable to invite them in, as I had chores to do before her return. That day, at her dialysis treatment, she died of cardiac arrest. "Hasta pronto, mi amor," she called out weakly on that last day of her life. Someday, surely, I will say to my son and granddaughter those words, too: "Until soon, my loves."

The occasion when my mother last sang to me comes to mind. I was leaving home—again—at age nineteen. She didn't know where I was off to or with whom. As if it were just yesterday, I can see my mamá at her desk where she used to pay bills, sort out Avon orders, and make an occasional telephone call. Because I saw her there a thousand times over twenty years, her dark profile and wavy hair are a cameo before my mind's eye. I see her right hand making notes. It was all so long ago, yet indelible.

That evening, although she may have feared for me and her fear always showed itself as disapproval, my mother made no scene to prevent my departure. Instead, as I closed the door of her flat and walked slowly down the hallway stairs, I heard a popular ballad issuing from her, "Paloma Negra." When I was a small child, one of my mother's pet names for me was Palomita Blanca. Apparently, the little white dove grew to be a big black one.

"I don't know whether to curse you or pray for you," the song goes, "You shouldn't play with my pride. Since your affection should have been mine and no one else's."

My mother's voice was loud and strong. It sent shudders through me, but I kept running down the stairs and out into the street.

It is the song I request of mariachis because we pay them to make us cry. And nothing can make you weep more than remembering when and how you left your mother's side, or, perhaps, the day she let you go.

Me in Chicago (1981).

Coda

I am not a political scientist or a historian, but a poet. Poets
are notorious for our grave opinions on the matters of all
things. My poet's ideals have led me to run an online zine,
La Tolteca, whose motto is promoting the advancement of a
world without borders or censorship. Ten years ago, teaching in Chicago one brutal winter too many, I left and made
my home near the US-Mexican border. The winters there
are not as fierce, but they can get cold, especially out in the
desert or in the mountains.

Many years ago I was invited to participate in an event at
the United Nations on women and literacy. There was at that
time a lot of enthusiasm over my novel *So Far from God*, about
a single mother with four daughters in New Mexico. Frus-
trated and despairing whether life could ever improve for
her, the mother runs for mayor of her village. I was honored
that my novel was selected for such an important venue, but
at some point it was noted at the UN that despite my name
and the book they had selected, I was not Mexican. New

Mexico became a part of the union in 1912 as part of that Manifest Destiny thing and, thus, I was an American. The American writer they had already chosen was the wonderful Grace Paley, so they proceeded to identify an academic and writer who made her life in the United States but was born in South America to represent Latinas. There was no place for a US Latina writing about ancestral lands now part of the United States. I was uninvited.

Today, we still have the difficulty of accepting that we are all here together, that human beings will migrate—by foot, train, raft, or ship—to form new communities and economies. No ethnic group en masse is ever freeloading. All people everywhere at some time endure the challenges of survival. We remain hopeful for humanity as a whole, even as we reluctantly contemplate the consequences of human impact on this earth.

What connects us—not just as citizens from so many walks of life, but to our past and future? Our stories. Day to day, we each form our own narratives of survival, of love, of family. I've dedicated my life to forming my stories, which I hope, above all, you have enjoyed.

Credits

My Mother's México (p. 11). Originally published in *Latina: Women's Voices from the Borderlands*, edited by Lillian Castillo-Speed, New York: Touchstone Books, 1995.

Remembering Las Cartoneras (p. 27). A version of this essay originally appeared in *FS: Feminist Studies*, vol. 34, issues 1–2 (Spring/Summer), 2008.

Her Last Tortillas (p. 45). Originally published in *MORE* magazine as "My Mother's Last Meal" in March 2009.

Bowing Out (p. 89). Originally published in *Salon*, April 12, 1999.

When I Died in Oaxaca (p. 117). First appeared in *Literature and Arts of the Americas*, vol. 36, issue 67, 2003.

Are Hunters Born or Made? (p. 131). Originally published in *Because I Said So*, edited by Camille Peri and Kate Moses, New York: HarperCollins, 2005.

Swimming with Sharks (p. 143). A version of this story was presented at the Moth as part of the PEN World Voices Festival in New York in 2008.

Acknowledgements

The essays in this collection were written over a span of more than twenty years. Mi mamá was still in the world when I first composed the essay "My Mother's México." Her departure came just a few years later. I dedicate these memories first to my small, dark, formidable mamá. As the expression goes, I became the woman I am today because of the mother and woman she was to me.

As a storyteller and a poet, I hope my stories serve to lift the spirits of my son, Marcel Castillo, and his daughter, my beloved nieta and namesake, Mariana Castillo, in years to come.

It is with deep appreciation that I recognize the Feminist Press. This project had a lot of starts and stops over the years. Amy Scholder, the former editorial director, listened without judgment when I spoke to her by phone to say why I could not write the essays I had promised to deliver. At that time, my heart was shattered. Instead, (and by way of mending, perhaps) I started a novel and the Feminist Press welcomed it. I thank the entire staff for their affection and support. Jennifer Baumgardner, as executive director and my editor, has given my work a home.

Lastly, I wrote the introductory essay as a lecture, part of my obligations as the Lund-Gil Endowed Chair at Dominican University outside Chicago. I was to address the Obama administration's Deferred Action for Childhood Arrivals (DACA) initiative. In the course of writing the lecture I traced my own family's migrations. The North American Invasion of 1846–48 changed the fate of Mexicans in the north and south of the new resultant border—then and through the present. Were it not for my mother's courage to migrate north to Chicago, it is nearly certain that I would not be writing these lines now. It is likely I would have followed in her footsteps and become a domestic servant in México. All labor has virtue, but I would not have had the voice I developed in Chicago, growing up in the heat of the civil rights movement.

The Feminist Press is a nonprofit educational organization founded to amplify feminist voices. FP publishes classic and new writing from around the world, creates cutting-edge programs, and elevates silenced and marginalized voices in order to support personal transformation and social justice for all people.

See our complete list of books at
feministpress.org

ANA CASTILLO is one of the most powerful and celebrated voices in contemporary Chicana literature. She is the author of *So Far from God* and *Sapogonia*, both *New York Times* Notable Books of the Year, as well as *The Guardians*, *Peel My Love Like an Onion*, and many other books of fiction, poetry, and essays. Her newest novel, *Give It to Me*, won a 2014 Lambda Literary Award; her seminal collection *Massacre of the Dreamers: Essays on Xicanisma* was rereleased as a twentieth anniversary edition in November 2014; and the award-winning *Watercolor Women, Opaque Men* will be rereleased in a new edition in the fall of 2016 by Northwestern University Press.